# SPITFIRE
## STORIES

# SPITFIRE
# STORIES

TRUE TALES FROM THOSE WHO DESIGNED,
MAINTAINED AND FLEW THE ICONIC PLANE

JACKY HYAMS

Michael O'Mara Books Limited

First published in Great Britain in 2017 by
Michael O'Mara Books Limited
9 Lion Yard
Tremadoc Road
London SW4 7NQ

'Sisters in Spitfires' and 'Model Pilot, Model Lawn' from *Sisters in Spitfires* (2015), reproduced by kind permission of Alison Hill.

A CIP catalogue record for this book is available from the British Library.

Papers used by Michael O'Mara Books Limited are natural, recyclable products made from wood grown in sustainable forests. The manufacturing processes conform to the environmental regulations of the country of origin.

ISBN: 978-1-78243-816-8 in hardback print format
ISBN: 978-1-78243-817-5 in ebook format

2 3 4 5 6 7 8 9 10

Designed and typeset by K. DESIGN www.k-design.org.uk

Printed and bound by CPI Group (UK) Ltd, Croydon, CR0 4YY

Every reasonable effort has been made to acknowledge all copyright holders. Any errors or omissions that may have occurred are inadvertent, and anyone with any copyright queries is invited to write to the publisher, so that a full acknowledgement may be included in subsequent editions of this work.

www.mombooks.com

*This book is dedicated to the many millions of ordinary people who 'did their bit' in the Second World War, especially the RAF ground staff and the Spitfire factory workers – the backroom creators of the legend.*

# Contents

# Foreword

*Flying Officer Geoffrey Wellum (right), with Flight
Lieutenant Brian Kingcome, next to a Spitfire at
Biggin Hill, 1941.*

THE FIRST TIME I EVER SAW a Spitfire, the voice of
authority bade me to go out there and fly it, and on no
account break it. Straight out of flight training with only
146 hours' total flying experience, of which 95 were solo,
I might have been forgiven for viewing the situation with
a certain degree of apprehension. But there she stood –
graceful, elegant and relaxed.

Once strapped into the cockpit, the Spitfire somehow had a friendly atmosphere about it, albeit a little confined. Nevertheless, I felt immediately part and parcel of the aeroplane and totally at ease. It was then that I realized what a privilege it was to have been chosen to fly one at such a crucial time in our history.

The view forward from the cockpit was restricted to say the least, due to the long nose and the narrow undercarriage, which gave it an unstable feeling during taxiing. But once in the air it was an entirely different matter. She was a thing transformed – light and responsive to every control input, the Spitfire seemed to slip through the air.

There were no vices and it became quite obvious to me what a truly magnificent design it was for a single-seater fighter aircraft. It says so much for the whole design concept of the Spitfire that when a young and impressionable pilot of nineteen, direct from training, could get into one, fly it in combat and in most cases make a safe return. It cannot be overstressed how fortunate it was that Spitfires arrived in squadron service just in time for the Second World War.

There has been much written concerning the iconic Spitfire, but *Spitfire Stories* approaches the subject from a refreshingly different angle, and I wish it every success.

*Geoffrey Wellum*
*92 Squadron – Biggin Hill*

# Introduction

THE IMAGE IS ICONIC AND THE history one of wartime victory against the odds. Yet in many ways, the advent of the Supermarine Spitfire was a minor miracle in itself.

The authorities of the early to mid-1930s could not be accused of having any sense of urgency when it came to developing Britain's air defences, or re-arming after the First World War in the event that another world war could be possible. The First World War was often described as 'the war to end all wars', and its brutality and horror left governments terrified at the prospect of further conflict. The 1930s was also a period of economic recession and unemployment in Britain; resources were scarce and most politicians did not wish to spend money on armaments. While Churchill saw the looming threat of Hitler's rise to power, many in the British government remained anti-war.

Britain's aviation industry was seriously under resourced and the Royal Air Force (RAF) had been greatly reduced in size, with very little being spent on aircraft development. Back in 1918, Britain had boasted the world's strongest air force. Yet by the early 1930s, the country was ranked fifth amongst the world's leading air powers. By the mid-1930s, the encroaching threat of war with Hitler's Germany could no longer be ignored: Germany was re-arming and the Luftwaffe was expanding at a much faster rate than the RAF. As a consequence, prototype new fighter planes – the Hurricane and the Supermarine Spitfire – were ordered for the RAF at the end of 1934. By the end of the 1930s it was obvious to many countries, including Britain, that Hitler had built up a mighty war machine.

The first Hurricane prototype took to the skies in November 1935, and the Supermarine Spitfire soon followed. The Spitfire's original designer, R. J. Mitchell, had designed many planes for aircraft manufacturer Supermarine by the time of its auspicious first ever test flight in March 1936 with Vickers Aviation's chief test pilot, Captain J. 'Mutt' Summers at the controls. Yet this was no instant success story: Mitchell's original design for a new fighter plane (dubbed 'The Shrew') designed to the exact specification of the Air Ministry, had originally been tested in February 1934 by Summers. Unfortunately, the plane's cooling system let it down and it failed to impress.

Undaunted, Mitchell returned to the drawing board. This time he bypassed the Air Ministry specifications to design a thinner elliptical wing, a smaller span and a cockpit with a Perspex cover. Plus, of course, a distinctive Rolls-Royce Merlin engine. His Spitfire plane wowed the watching air marshals and won the day. Yet although the successful Spitfire test flight – an acknowledged turning point in aviation history – led to a contract being issued in June that year for Supermarine to produce 310 Spitfires, the frontline operational strength of the RAF remained pitifully weak when compared to that of Germany's Luftwaffe, and it was not until 1940, after war had been declared, that Spitfire production really got going. Sadly, Mitchell never knew the true success of his inspirational design as he died just one year later from bowel cancer, aged only forty-two. A year later the Spitfire entered RAF Squadron service, delivered to 19 Squadron at Duxford. The subsequent development of the Spitfire from that initial Mark I pioneer through to twenty-four different Spitfire types or marks was due to the talents of the Supermarine team, headed by Joe Smith, Mitchell's successor as Chief Designer.

Even in those early war years, however, it had still been touch and go when it came to getting the plane off the production line: in May 1940, for instance, the Air Ministry came perilously close to cancelling orders because the Spitfire required a lot of hand-building and finishing, making it more costly than anticipated. But the orders were completed and, that same month, inspired by the efforts of Canadian media tycoon Lord Beaverbrook (Max Aitken), Spitfire fundraising to build the planes – £5,000 per Spitfire was the figure given at the time – took off at breakneck speed across Britain and around the world.

The general public had become increasingly aware of aviation, queuing up to watch air displays and willing to pay five shillings a time at flying circuses, where pilots toured the country and treated the paying public to a thrilling ride in their planes. While Hurricane fighter pilots shot down more enemy planes than the Spitfire and, indeed, more Hurricanes took to the skies in the Battle of Britain, it was the Supermarine Spitfire that captured the public's imagination, thanks in part to its glamorous ancestry via the famous float or seaplane air races of the 1930s such as the Schneider Trophy, the most prestigious annual trophy for such an event. The Supermarine seaplanes broke world speed records, winning the Schneider Trophy outright for Britain in 1933. Even before the Spitfire took centre stage in the Second World War, the Supermarine brand already implied a prestigious heritage of aviation superiority.

As soon as war was declared in September 1939, the Spitfire was up in the sky: in October 1939 an enemy aircraft was intercepted over Britain for the very first time and the Spitfire dominated the front pages as the first ever plane to tangle with the enemy.

Despite all the many restrictions of wartime, the Spitfire was frequently touted as the country's trump card to the millions of newspaper readers, a propaganda tool extraordinaire in an era without television where families crowded round their radio for news. Amidst the bombings and the fury of war, cinema audiences soared, too, and millions watched newsreels that gave brief glimpses of the war – and, sometimes, the Spitfire. The image of the plane itself became deeply embedded in the public consciousness.

By 1942 the general public was acutely conscious of the Spitfire's significance in the war effort. So when the story of the Spitfire and its development by R. J. Mitchell got the Hollywood treatment in *The First of the Few*, starring the biggest movie actors of the day, David Niven and Leslie Howard, this somewhat romanticized version of the plane's history delivered an even greater impact on audiences in Britain and America.

Even after war ended, the Spitfire retained its place in people's hearts. The legendary plane was now part of the national identity and films such as *Malta Story* (1953) starring Alec Guinness played a big part in drawing public attention to the Spitfire's role in Britain's history. Those Sunday afternoon movies in the age of huge TV audiences in the 1960s, 1970s and 1980s built solidly on that impact, working its way down through the generations.

In the twenty-first century, the love affair with the Spitfire remains undiminished. Almost eighty years later, the Spitfire retains a powerfully iconic status virtually unknown for any other aeroplane, a romantic emblem of a faraway era when Britain stood alone to fight off a mighty enemy, helped by an agile, curvy, elegant fighter plane with a distinctive elliptical oval wing and whining Merlin engine, piloted by the bravest of young men. Today, historic airshows and displays play a huge part in this, along with the Imperial War Museums and the RAF Museum, which allow the public to continue to enjoy the spectacle of these extraordinary fighters. Witness a Battle Proms Air Display Concert where a Spitfire swoops through the skies to the accompaniment of Elgar's *Nimrod* or similarly evocative music and try to ignore the flood of emotion it evokes.

Fifty airworthy Spitfires are still to be found across the globe. Recent relaxation of the regulations around pleasure flights in historic aircraft has also made a very big difference for Spitfire devotees, making it much easier for people to enjoy a pleasure flight in a Spitfire converted to a two-seat trainer: at the time of writing, ten different organizations in the UK offer a pleasure flight in a Spitfire to the general public.

Yet beneath the icon and its history, there remains another, equally fascinating story: that of the people behind the Spitfire. We tend to associate the Spitfire, quite naturally, with its wartime heroes: the RAF pilots from many countries who served through the war and beyond, flying the Spitfires and other planes, or 'The Few' of the Battle of Britain whose valiant efforts will never be forgotten.

Yet there are many others whose lives have been affected in some way by the Spitfire – the factory workers, the ground staff and the engineers, as well as the pilots and individuals whose love and passion for the Spitfire changed their lives. Such stories resonate down the years from wartime right to the present day.

There were over 20,400 Spitfires built during the Second World War in two key locations: Castle Bromwich in the West Midlands, and in the Southampton area, with 'shadow' factories producing aircraft and parts in buildings or areas specially converted to aircraft manufacturing dotted around the country. Thousands of Spitfire workers, many of them women who joined the 'secret army' of Britain's munitions workers, toiled in these factories, in often difficult conditions, as the country struggled to survive and work through the frequent bombing raids overhead.

Others were engaged in a wide range of Spitfire roles for the RAF and its wartime auxiliary organization, the Air Transport Auxiliary (ATA), whose female ferry pilots were the first women in the world to fly brand new Spitfires and other planes from factory to RAF airfield.

It is also a little acknowledged fact that it was the RAF ground crews, the 'erks' as they were called, who worked through the night and in difficult conditions to get the fighting Spitfires back up into battle. Their efforts, dedication and skills were a significant factor behind the RAF's success in the Battle of Britain. While they were relatively low in the pecking order, some 'erks' went on to become the best fighter pilots of the war. In that sense, in a country still rigidly class bound in wartime, the RAF itself became a meritocracy.

Every one of these many thousands of workers and their families played some part in this story of the Spitfire. This collection of stories, sourced from the archives of the Imperial War Museums, the RAF Museum, Solent Sky Museum, Southampton, as well as from interviews with wartime veterans and their families, reveals a glimpse of the hardship, pathos, humour and camaraderie of day-to-day life in wartime Britain – from the factory cleaner putting in a fifty-hour week for the 'good wages' of £2 a week to the Spitfire heroes taking to the skies in death-defying patrols while being filmed and feted by Hollywood's finest. Every story in this book reveals a unique connection to the iconic plane.

I have read a great deal about the way in which the British people committed themselves in wartime to 'doing their bit' on the home front, but it was something of a surprise to me to realize that this was no exaggeration – people during that period really did feel that each and every contribution to the war effort made a difference. While the Spitfire came at just the right time, an icon of excellence for a beleaguered nation in its darkest hour, we learn through these stories that it was the contribution of the people behind the plane, the teamwork, that truly gave the Spitfire its esteemed place in our history.

# CHAPTER 1

## A Star is Born

THE EARLY DAYS OF THE SPITFIRE brought with them some fascinating stories of the design and production of the iconic fighter plane. But at the heart of the Spitfire's history we find inspiration in a spirited young girl, and the generosity of the Great British public. Their love affair with the aircraft resulted in huge amounts of money being raised to keep the fighter in the air despite the hardships of wartime, and became an important symbol of national pride.

### Little Annie

1936 was a highly auspicious year for the Spitfire. It was the year of the fighter plane's first test flight, its first ever public appearance – and its first contract from the Air Ministry. Yet behind the scenes that year, an important decision had to be made: how should they name this exceptional new fighter?

The chairman at Vickers-Armstrongs (who had taken a controlling interest in the Supermarine Aviation works in 1928) was Sir Robert McLean. He had run the Indian railway system at the Great Indian Peninsula Railway and returned to Britain in 1929 to join the board of Vickers-Armstrongs, working closely with designer R. J. Mitchell on the development of the new plane as it progressed.

McLean believed the plane's name should begin with the letter 'S', to tie in with Supermarine. He also felt that the company's new fighter should, by its one-word name, suggest something super-powerful, a fiercely combative fighter. Mitchell put forward his own suggestions: Snipe? Scarab? What about Shrew? But McLean was unconvinced. And then an idea struck him.

'Little Spitfire' was a nickname McLean had given to his eldest daughter, Annie, when she was a child, a phrase commonly used at the time to describe a girl with a fiery personality. Toddler Annie had been a real livewire, a spirited and engaging extrovert who'd gone on to enjoy a career as an actor after she left school. McLean tried his new name out on the top brass at the Air Ministry. But it was now their turn to be sceptical, and Mitchell also had his reservations about the name, much preferring 'the Shrew'. Yet the chairman wasn't about to be put off. Instinct told him the plane should be called the Spitfire. It seemed the right description of what everyone hoped the new fighter would be capable of.

Mitchell's health, by then, was rapidly deteriorating: legend has it that on hearing of the final decision, he'd commented: 'It's just the bloody silly sort of name they would give it.' Early in 1937 Mitchell reluctantly gave up work. He died in June that year, unable to witness the Spitfire's success. Or learn how its name suited its performance perfectly.

As for Annie McLean, her own life took some extraordinary turns. On Christmas Eve of 1936 she married a handsome, divorced thirty-one-year-old English actor called Robert Newton after they met while Annie was working on voiceovers at the BBC. Six years her senior, Newton became well known in the 1950s for his film roles in *Treasure Island* and *Oliver Twist* and also enjoyed a successful stage career in the West End. Sadly, however, their marriage floundered amidst Newton's reputation for hard drinking and womanizing (the late hellraising actor Oliver Reed was reported to have regarded Robert Newton as a role model) and by the end of the war Annie had divorced him.

Yet her second marriage to Beakus Penrose proved far more successful. Penrose was the well-to-do ex-husband of Newton's sister Joy. In 1948, the newlyweds set up home in a large eighteenth-century house called Killiow, near Truro. The house had once been home to eighteenth-century English painter Sir Joshua Reynolds's niece, Theophila. Set in some 300 acres of parkland, and with a large farm, the house became a major restoration project for the couple. Annie relished the challenge, creating a stunning estate garden which duly specialized in selling up to a hundred varieties of camellia. Here, in Cornwall, 'Little Spitfire' found peace and contentment, raising two sons and enjoying life to the full.

After Beakus died in 1988 and despite her advancing years, Annie remained at Killiow, helping develop the area into a country park and an eighteen-hole golf course. Right to the end of her life, Annie Penrose loved to cook and entertain her many friends from the theatrical world. Declaring the opening of the estate to the public each spring, she became a much-loved local sight, sitting atop a shire horse and blowing a hunting horn. Yet her Spitfire past never left her: she maintained her close connection over the years and became an Honorary Member of the Spitfire Society.

As part of the celebrations for her 100th birthday in 2010 in Falmouth, a Spitfire fly-past was organized, trailing a banner wishing Spitfire Annie a happy 100th birthday. She died in October 2011, aged 101.

## The Spitfire Fund

The British public's love affair with the Spitfire resulted in huge sums of money being raised for the war effort. Winston Churchill's newly appointed Minister of Aircraft Production, the Canadian newspaper tycoon Max Aitken, Lord Beaverbrook ('The Beaver'), spearheaded the idea of making public appeals to gather donations of raw materials that could help the war effort. Combined with the huge press coverage of the Spitfire and the public's desire to get involved, the initial idea of asking people to donate their pots and pans 'to help build Spitfires' very quickly turned into a Spitfire fundraising campaign.

The nominal 'price' of a Spitfire was set at £5,000 (around £300,000 nowadays), though the true cost of building one was closer to three times that amount. Within a matter of weeks, all kinds of Spitfire funds were set up by local councils, businesses and charities, as well as individuals – many coordinated by local newspapers carrying lists of individual donations. Auctions and raffles were popular crowd-pullers. Very soon the BBC broadcast lists of successful funds at the end of news broadcasts and virtually every big town in Britain got involved. Old and young, wealthy and poor – the miners of Durham, already struggling with high unemployment – donated funds for two Spitfires. The idea of raising the cash to contribute towards building a Spitfire had hit a nerve in the public psyche at just the right moment.

The idea that every penny donated counted was highlighted by the publication of a components price list: £2,000 raised would buy a Spitfire wing; £200 bought a gun; eight shillings bought a spark plug; sixpence could buy a rivet.

Newspaper stories of the time reflected the novelty and humour of the endeavour. For example, one story revealed that a farmer in Kent charged locals sixpence 'to see the only field in Kent without a German aircraft in it'. In another, during an air raid, a London cinema manager pushed a wheelbarrow up and down the aisle asking: 'The more you give, the less raids there will be'. A Liverpool 'lady of the night' donated £3 at the police station 'for the Spitfire Fund' (£3 was the standard fine for soliciting at the time). And in Market Lavington, Wiltshire, an outline of a Spitfire was drawn in the market square. Locals were asked to fill it with coins. It was filled within a few days.

Fundraisers were also given the opportunity to have their dedication of choice painted onto a Spitfire, and in many cases the aircraft were named after the places or areas that had successfully raised the money. Eventually, almost every big town in Britain came to have its name on a Spitfire.

Efforts grew and soon the fundraising went global, with Canada and other Commonwealth countries joining the effort. This was kickstarted by Garfield Weston, a Canadian businessman and philanthropist who was also a Conservative MP for Macclesfield at the time. In August 1940, after a day of heavy losses in the Battle of Britain, with sixteen Spitfires lost in one battle and thirteen pilots killed, Weston walked into the Ministry of Aircraft Production and handed fellow Canadian, Lord Beaverbrook, a blank cheque saying: 'You know, Max, only God can replace those boys. I'd like to replace the machines.' Beaverbrook filled in the amount for £100,000. Weston hoped to keep the donation a secret, but it was soon made clear to him that this simply wasn't possible. As Beaverbrook explained, the publicity generated by his gesture would raise further sums of cash.

On 24 August, another Canadian tycoon, J. W. McConnell, publisher of the *Montreal Star*, put up 1 million Canadian dollars. Garfield Weston took to the airwaves in a broadcast aired over the BBC and CBS radio networks. 'The princely gift from an outstanding Canadian made all England stand and cheer,' he said, prompting a huge wave of additional Canadian Spitfire fundraising ventures. One of the most entertaining of these became the Dorothy Funds.

Dorothy Christie of Montreal launched the idea by auctioning off some of her evening wear, using the money she made to print cards that said: 'Is your name Dorothy? If so, rally round and help buy a Spitfire for Britain.' She and a group of friends then mailed the cards to every Dorothy they could find. This relatively simple idea spawned 20,000 fundraising tea parties (all hosted by a Dorothy) and Dorothy-inspired sales, musicals and even an auction of one of movie star Dorothy Lamour's famous sarongs. This eventually resulted in a Spitfire being named 'Dorothy of Great Britain and Empire'.

Donations to Spitfire Funds raised around £13 million. Technically, however, the money raised by the Spitfire funds went towards the war effort in general, rather than directly to the aircraft manufacturers. Yet Beaverbrook, the *Daily Express* newspaper tycoon of the era, was very well placed as a Fleet Street baron to stimulate public interest by deploying the Spitfire as a hugely emotive cause.

It has been argued that Beaverbrook's inspiration to use the Spitfire as a fundraising model was really a highly effective propaganda exercise in creating patriotism: people believed that the country could win the war because it had the Spitfire. Yet Beaverbrook was the man who increased Britain's fighter and bomber aircraft production, after the problems of how to mass produce the planes was solved, took control of RAF storage units and aircraft repairs, and injected energy and resourcefulness into a situation where such skills were desperately needed. Britain needed hope, and belief in the country's future; the fundraising efforts gave millions of people just that.

# THE SHEPLEY SPITFIRE

It was the happiest of wartime summer weddings when twenty-one-year-old Pilot Officer Douglas Shepley married Frances 'Bidy' Linscott on 29 June 1940 in Sidcup, Kent. Douglas Shepley had graduated from Cranwell at the start of the war and joined 152 Squadron at Acklington, Northumberland, moving to Warmwell, Dorset, just a few weeks after his wedding day.

Shepley was no stranger to loss despite his young age. His sister, Jeanne, had died in North Africa in 1939 after joining the FANY (First Aid Nursing Yeomanry) when her ship, the SS *Yorkshire*, sailing from Rangoon to Liverpool, was torpedoed. It sank, killing sixty passengers. In May the following year, Shepley's brother George was shot down over Dunkirk while on a reconnaissance sortie. Fate, it seemed, had the Shepley family in its sight. On 12 August, during the Battle of Britain, Shepley's Spitfire and that of Australian Flight Lieutenant Latham Withall fell into the sea near the Isle of Wight in combat during the Luftwaffe's sortie to put British radar stations out of action.

Their bodies were never found. Yet Douglas' widow, Bidy, after just six weeks of marriage, was determined to honour her late husband. Together with her mother-in-law, Emily, she vowed to raise the money to replace the Spitfire her husband had been flying. With fundraising collections in all the ARP (Air Raid Precaution) posts in the Sheffield area, the determined duo managed to raise £5,700 in less than four months.

Afterwards, Lord Beaverbrook wrote to Emily Shepley: 'Will you allow me, in sending you my heartfelt sympathy in the tragic losses you have sustained, to tell you how proud I am. I am convinced your sons and daughter would be proud to know of the tribute you have paid in their memory.'

A year later, in August 1941, a new Spitfire, a Mark Vb, named 'The Shepley Spitfire', was issued to 602 (City of Glasgow) Squadron. Sadly, it was lost in March 1942 while being flown by Battle of Britain veteran, Group Captain Victor Beamish, DSO, DFC. Yet the Spitfire continued to linger in the memory of the Shipley family.

In 1979, the Shepley Spitfire pub opened in Totley, just outside Sheffield, near the Shepley family home – a monument to those that built and flew the Spitfire and the family who were determined to turn tragedy into hope.

## First Flight

Gordon Bailey was sixteen when he went to work in an aircraft factory in 1936. 'It was a rather special one in those days – Supermarine Aviation Works on the River Itchen at Woolston, Southampton. Some years earlier a very famous aircraft was designed and built at these works. It was world famous. The Schneider Trophy float plane had finally won the contest outright for Britain.'

Initially, Gordon found himself working two to a bench

on template details for the Walrus and Stranraer biplanes (or flying boats). 'For the first week I was somewhat in awe of factory work but this feeling soon wore off and I began to enjoy work and the routine. It was very strict in pre-war days. Work to the bell had to be strictly observed, pass-outs obtained to leave early and no smoking, though this was no hardship to the youngest of us.

'On our section, a charge hand supervised over about forty lads of my own age, with one or two older men for the more skilled jobs. The general foreman was a terror to almost everyone, especially us lads. A dreaded punishment for misbehaviour was to be taken to the main floor, issued with a hacksaw and about a dozen blades. A long dural block was then marked off by the toolmakers and the lad earmarked for punishment was set the job of sawing, with a demanded standard of accuracy, the whole length of it. This certainly made us think more than twice about stepping out of line in working hours.

'Just around that time we heard about a new aeroplane that was being planned and built by Supermarine. An aeroplane quite different from the ones in service at that time, it was all semi-secret and a bit vague. But when one day I chanced to see it for the first time, I knew somehow that this was something entirely new and exciting and very beautiful, if such a term can be used about an aeroplane.

'A small section of the works was boarded off and a team of fitters, draughtsmen and planners were busy on its construction. I had to go to one of the fitters one morning to borrow a tool for the man I was working with and then had a chance to see it.

'There it was on trestles, a low-winged monoplane, slim and beautifully shaped. It certainly was a unique design for that time, and it looked a winner from the start.

'Several months went by, until one day something happened that would alter things for me considerably. One morning I was talking to another boy on a bench not far from mine when I felt, rather than saw, someone standing behind me. Oh no, it was the general foreman, the terror himself. What next? I thought to myself. I soon found out. I was told off in no uncertain terms for being out of my workplace. This was driven home by the use of some swear words. I don't know why I said it but I told him that I was wrong to be out of my place but I also didn't like being sworn at. This evidently sealed matters, for a few minutes later I was sacked and would leave Supermarine that very evening. This was a blow.

'I settled down to wait for five o'clock rather than work. As usual at the sound of the knock-off whistle, the queue formed for wages. It was the custom for the general foreman, the terror himself, to stand by the pay clerk while each man received his pay. At last it was my turn. As I received my envelope, I was curtly told by the foreman to stand aside and wait, which I did. After the men dwindled and left I was called to the window. "Your name is Bailey?" It was the foreman.

"Yes, sir," I replied.

"You're the one I've sacked, aren't you?"

"Yes, sir."

"You said you didn't like being sworn at as well as being told off," he said.

"That's right," I managed to get out.

'As near a smile as we had ever seen started to appear on his face, only to vanish at once. "How would you like to go to Eastleigh Airport to work instead?" he asked.

'What a question to ask. I certainly would, a thousand times yes. The following Monday I started work at Eastleigh.

'Top and bottom main planes were being assembled there and I was put as fitter's mate on top planes. We were working in an old hangar that had been built by German POWs in the First World War. The aerodrome wasn't very busy in those days. The Hampshire Aeroplane Club was in operation on a small scale and Imperial Airways operated from there, but not on a large scale. We had two or three Walrus Fleet Air Arm aircraft a week come from Woolston for test flight and inspection. It was a nice self-contained unit with an adjoining hangar where Supermarine kept a few planes stored and maintained. Two aircraft we had there were the Avro Tudor and the Hawker Tomtit (biplanes used as training planes). They were used by our test pilots to ferry them between the various units operated by the firm.

'Some time midway through 1936 a new hangar was erected at the south end of the aerodrome, a new Flight Shed for Supermarine, which was merged into Vickers and was in future known as Vickers Supermarine Aviation. Also at this time, a small notice in our local *Echo* told of the moving of a new fighter aircraft from Woolston to Eastleigh. The Spitfire soon arrived and was installed in a corner of our hangar. The little aeroplane was painted blue all over and numbered K5054. It was the first prototype proper of the Spitfire Mk I.

'A Rolls-Royce Merlin of 1,050 horsepower, a two-blade fixed-pitch prop and tail skid were fitted and RAF roundels were added to wings and fuselage. A couple of months were to go by before she was ready to fly. But at least it was on an aerodrome and in one piece. I was able to see it at leisure, and properly.

'Very soon, things were moving in our hangar. The tiny Spitfire's first flight was just around the corner. It had been inspected and checked time after time in the last few months and we heard everything was set for the word go. "Right," I thought, "I'm going to be present, come what may." When she was pushed out onto the tarmac, I intended to be one of the pushers. Our foreman was fully occupied, so I was okay there. So, after fixing it with my fitter, I helped push K5054 out and then "lose" myself outside the hangar. It was a nice, typical March day, a good ceiling and not a lot of wind. I kept discreetly out of the way, watching and waiting for the big moment.

'Around the Spitfire there was a fair old gathering of Air Ministry officials, Supermarine officials and the necessary fitters to stand by for last minute adjustments. After a while K5054 was "tied down" for its pre-flight ground run. This was the job of the Rolls-Royce representative attached to Supermarine. At last all was ready and with a puff of smoke from its exhausts the Merlin started its warm up. The flight was nearly on. A few minutes later the Rolls man was evidently satisfied with the temperatures and started to run her at a quicker tempo. Louder and louder roared the Merlin till it reached its peak, held for a moment or two, then gradually died down to a very smooth tick-over. He was evidently pleased and switched off. The Merlin's prop spun to a stop and the ground run was over.

'We all thought that Supermarine's Chief Test Pilot would have the honour of piloting it for the first time. He was Mr Jeffrey Quill, a great pilot. But it was not to be. Vickers' Chief, in view of seniority, was to take her first and then hand over to our Mr Quill. This was all very proper, no doubt, but to me it was a disappointment. In a short while, Mr Summers was strapped into the tiny cockpit, started the Merlin and without further ado taxied out to the take-off point at the southern end of the aerodrome.

As he turned into the wind, he opened up the Merlin of K5054 and the life of the immortal Spitfire had started. With a roar, the little aeroplane shot forward, tail up and raring to go. After a reasonable run she was airborne, wheels up, engine sounding powerful and sweet. Mr Summers eased her into the blue and in no time was out of our sight. After a short flight he came in sight; swept across the aerodrome, a left-hand circuit, wheels down, and came in to land. The Spitfire had come to stay.'

# CHAPTER 2

# Making an Icon

IN 1936, THE BRITISH GOVERNMENT FORMALIZED the shadow factory plan under the control of the Air Ministry to increase aircraft production, employing tens of thousands of factory workers across the country. Despite the dark days of war, the camaraderie of the workers and the feeling of 'doing your bit' for Britain inspired many of those involved in the production of the Spitfire, and they look back with fondness and pride on an extraordinary time.

## A Spitfire Made from Half a Crown

As the Battle of Britain raged across the skies in the late summer of 1940, Germany's Luftwaffe were determined to destroy the main Spitfire manufacturing sites at Woolston and Itchen, in Southampton's suburbs.

Their first attempt on 23 August proved unsuccessful. Yet later raids the following month were devastating: the two main sites were completely wrecked, killing ninety-two and injuring many others. Many of the casualties worked on the production line.

Fortunately, plans had already been made to relocate some

of the two factories' production equipment and machine tools elsewhere in the Southampton area. In addition, factories in other areas of the country were commissioned by the government to continue the production of the Spitfire. These were known as secret or 'shadow' factories, and in Salisbury, Wiltshire, many garages and even furniture stores were converted in order to continue building the Spitfires around the clock.

Many of the employees of these shadow factories were local young women like Dot Rendell, who had grown up in Marden, near Devizes, and started her working life in service for a local doctor and his wife. 'The Germans were already dropping incendiary bombs near the house,' recalled Dot. 'Our fear was that the bombers would follow, but they didn't.'

Dot was just seventeen when war broke out, and her first ever boyfriend was a sailor who served on the *Ark Royal*, Britain's most famous aircraft carrier. 'It was more of a correspondence course than a romance, but he lived locally and appreciated letters home.'

By late 1940, Vickers-Armstrongs, the owners of Supermarine Aviation Works, had evacuated production to thirty-five sites in the Trowbridge, Southampton, Reading and Newbury areas, as well as to Salisbury, Wiltshire. They occupied Anna Valley Garage and Dorset Garages in Castle Street as well as Wessex Motors in New Street. A new factory was also built in Castle Road and thousands of young women began working in these sites and the other shadow sites dotted around the country. Dot was one of them. Initially, she worked in stock keeping in stores at the

Wessex Motors site. Then she transferred to the shop floor to help build the Spitfires.

'We used a Cardex system with separate pull-out files for every item in the store. Our job was to record every intake and output and then report any shortages to the "chaser" [a man who scoured the country for much needed parts].' In time, Dot became friendly with a girl there who worked as an electrician. 'So when the opportunity arose I joined her on the shop floor. We fitted electric instruments to the dashboards and Oddie clips [a quick-release fastener used widely in the aviation industry at the time] throughout the fuselage to hold wiring. It was all very different to the quiet I was used to!

'We were not trained for electrical work, we did not connect any wires. We were given a blueprint to follow. If we did have problems, the charge hand helped us out. The Oddie clips were various sizes, depending on the number of wires they were meant to hold. We had to position them and drill holes ready for the riveters. Not much space in the tail of a Spitfire, so it was an advantage to be small! The dashboard instruments were fitted and riveted in the same way.

'*Music While You Work* echoed through the factory and everyone would join in the chorus of "We'll Meet Again" with Vera Lynn, endeavouring to be heard above the panel beating and riveting.'

But despite the seemingly carefree atmosphere, the workers were very aware of the reason they were all there and the important work they were carrying out. 'We had an air raid shelter deep under the floor, which we used when sirens sounded. Everyone carried their gas masks at all times.'

There was a factory canteen for the workers. 'They took over the area above Smith's News Agency shop for the canteen and we had social functions there like staff dances. The excellent three-man band were factory workers. We had super times there. There were lots of on-off romances in the factory. I had friends but no serious involvements.

'My treasured keepsake from those factory days is a Spitfire made out of half a crown. We were all given one as a gift when the war ended.'

## Dead Sea

A few months after the Battle of Britain, Paul Nash, one of a small number of official war artists appointed by the Air Ministry in 1940, moved to Oxford with his wife Margaret. Nash was fascinated by a huge depot located in Cowley, east of Oxford. As a surrealist artist of considerable repute, Nash had already witnessed the worst of the First World War and created stunningly powerful abstract works such as *We Are Making a New World*, completed in 1918. Now, at Cowley, he started to create a fresh work of art in order to boost patriotic sentiment. And his inspiration was Cowley's enormous aircraft salvage dump, nothing more than piles and piles of twisted, damaged metal.

Previously part of the Morris car factory, Cowley had been turned into a salvage and recycling operation called the Metal Produce Recovery Unit as part of the war effort.

Spread over 100 acres and employing over 1,500 men and women, the unit was tasked with recovering damaged planes, including Spitfires and crashed German fighter aircraft, from anywhere in the UK and bringing them to Cowley for repair or recycling. A similar recovery unit was also set up in the north-east of England, at Eaglescliffe, sited at an old brickworks by a railway line. Here, too, all crashed and unrepairable planes from across the north of England came to be stripped of all reusable parts and smelted down to recover aluminium by a further team of 1,500 workers.

Nash's war artist contemporaries such as Eric Kennington painted conventional portraits of Battle of Britain fighter pilots, using pastels to create glamorous, dashing figures in blue RAF uniform, or, in the case of artist Cuthbert Orde, a series of black and white drawings of pilots in Fighter Command, both styles fulfilling the image the Air Ministry was very keen to promote. But Paul Nash found himself intrigued by the Cowley site and these junked planes that had fought so fiercely in the air.

The depot got so big, parts of the area were given names like Spitfire Road and Battle Road and Nash spent several months at Cowley sketching and photographing the seemingly endless piles of wrecked, twisted metal, commenting on the ghostly presence of the crashed planes, sensing a pervasive, eerie presence around the site. At one stage he called the planes 'beautiful monsters'. 'One could swear they begin to move and twist and turn as they did in the air,' he said afterwards, describing his oil on canvas landscape of a moonlit landscape of crashed German planes. At first glance, what might seem to be moonlit waves proves to be an unending expanse of wreckage of Second World War aircraft, a painting Nash named *Totes Meer* (German for 'Dead Sea').

As unusual as his work at Cowley was, *Totes Meer* was subsequently regarded as a very effective piece of war propaganda. That he succeeded in producing some of the greatest images of the Second World War until his death, aged fifty-seven, just after war ended in 1946, is a testament to his determination – Nash was severely asthmatic and his illness often proved debilitating. In his unconventional way, Nash brilliantly conveyed the terrible power of war, inspired by the sight of a vast expanse of twisted, unwanted metal.

## Making Spitfires in Castle Bromwich

### Eileen Weston's story

Spitfire production in the Second World War was split between two sites: Southampton and the surrounding areas of 'shadow' factories, and at the vast Castle Bromwich aircraft factory near Birmingham.

Thousands of factory workers were employed at the Castle Bromwich site through the war years, making the planes and parts so urgently needed by the RAF. Some of these workers were young teenage girls, drafted in to help with the war effort.

'We all knew we were doing something important,' recalls Eileen Weston, eldest of six children, who lived in Erdington, close to the Castle Bromwich factory. She left school aged fourteen, just one month before war was declared. She'd had dreams of going to art school. But times were hard for her family and there was only one option: find a job.

'Castle Bromwich were advertising for staff,' said Eileen. 'I wanted to work in the drawing office but there were no vacancies. But they said they would be prepared to train me on what they called the cashier machines. This involved using what was called the Hollerith system, which was a very early form of punched card data processing, so I could help prepare the wages for their accounts section.'

Eileen was sent to a training centre in Birmingham to learn how to use the machines. For a fourteen-year-old going into the workplace, it was not the easiest of transitions. 'I'd get home and cry at night because the supervisor was so strict, it was terrible: "WHY are you looking at the clock?", that sort of thing, all the time. But I managed to learn what was needed.'

Starting work at the huge factory site with its many separate noisy buildings was initially quite awesome. 'You clocked in each day and you had to show your passbook to get in. I kept mine – more as a reminder of myself at fourteen than anything else. Never having had a job before, it seemed very strange at first but, of course, actually working in a place where they were building these amazing Spitfires we'd read about in the papers was quite something.

'When I first went through the place and actually saw them all making the planes, the women all wearing turbans, singing at the tops of their voices, I thought "How can they work with all this noise?" But you soon got used to it all.'

Eileen's working hours in accounts were nine to five each day plus Saturday morning, and the wage was ten shillings a week. 'It went up, but slowly. One Christmas, they gave us all extra money. I suppose it was some sort of productivity bonus. I found a white five-pound note in my paypacket, which to me was incredible. I thought I was the richest person I knew!'

The threat of attack, however, was constant. One morning Eileen arrived at work to discover that one of the factory blocks had been hit in an air raid. 'A lot of people had been killed. We were issued with tin hats and told that if the alarm went off, to just get under the metal desks. They thought we wouldn't have time to get to the shelters if it was a sudden attack.' Such was the concern about air attacks, at one stage Eileen found herself evacuated with the other accounts people to work at Sutton Coldfield, a nearby suburb. 'A coach would take us from the factory each day to Far End, in the Four Oaks area, where there were lots of very big houses. About fifty of us would be bussed there every morning to do the work and then they'd drive us back again in the evening.'

The work itself was monotonous, punching wages information onto a card that then went into various sorting machines. 'My day would be spent pressing out numbers. I didn't think too much about the information, how much people earned. At that age you're not particularly interested in that sort of thing. But the section where I worked was very friendly. There might be air raids but you took it all in your stride.'

On weekends, there would be big dances organized for factory staff. Like so many vast munitions factories, it was essential for the workers to have some sort of entertainment and break from what was essentially a relentless working routine on the production line, with the ever-present threat of air raid warnings. 'There were always far more men than women at those dances,' recalled Eileen. 'The place was always packed with servicemen, many of them based nearby at RAF Lichfield, so you'd start dancing with someone for a few steps, then there'd be a tap on the shoulder with another one wanting to dance.'

As routine as the day-to-day work was, being in the midst of such a huge enterprise engaged in building the Spitfires did carry with it a sense of pride in 'doing their bit'. 'You could see where the wings were being made in one section, the painting in another. Watching the planes being wheeled out to the airfield was the big thrill for all of us. If you were in your break, you might stand and watch them being tested. But you couldn't stop work just to watch them fly. We were all very well supervised. In those days, you did what you were told!

'Of course, like everyone else I was hoping for the war to end, but when it did come I realized the factory would be wound up, and then what would I do?' Eileen needn't have worried. With her wartime experience, it was easy to get another job in the accounts section of Joseph Lucas, a nearby car accessories firm. She worked there until she got married in 1951 and started a family.

What always stood out most of all in Eileen's memory was the friendly camaraderie between all the workers. 'It was a kind of fellowship, knowing we were all doing something so important. You'd walk through the factory and chat with people. Everyone seemed to get on. You never saw anyone rowing or getting upset,' she recalled. 'Those ladies in their turbans, singing at the top of their voices while they worked – it really was a fantastic atmosphere.'

## TAKE COVER

Eileen kept an interdepartmental memo from Air Commodore R. H. Verney, retired RAF Director of Technical Development, and a former First World War aviator. Dated 29 August 1940, the printed note was handed out to all workers in her section. It makes for interesting reading.

### ACTION TO BE TAKEN IN THE EVENT OF A SURPRISE AIR RAID BY DAY

(a)   The private alarm (buzzer) in each block will be sounded and this will be the signal to take cover against a wall, machine tool or under the bench, as convenient, but not to evacuate the block.

(b)   In the case of any of the buzzers failing to act properly, or in the case of A and B blocks, which are not yet provided with buzzers, the signal to take cover will be given by a series of long blasts on a whistle, given by the Superintendent or Foreman.

(c)   The Superintendent will then decide whether to evacuate the block or not.

In this he may be guided by information from the Control Office by seeing the probable scale of attack from outside or both. If he decides to evacuate, he will give the signal with a series of short blasts on the whistle.

(d) He will keep one whistle himself, and allot others to foremen and ARP Wardens at his discretion. He will instruct them that they should be prepared to give the 'Take Cover' signal on their own initiative on hearing the sound of a bomb explosion or any probable indication of attack. [The above was explained with the aid of the loud speaker van, at a meeting of employees on the 24 August at 2 p.m. at which the best method of avoiding injury with only partial cover was demonstrated, viz: to lie flat on the face with the palms of the hands closing the ears, and the fingers clasped together round the neck.]

(e) If the public alarm is sounded this procedure will not apply and evacuation will proceed in the normal manner but if circumstances in their opinion necessitate it, Superintendents may apply it and give the 'Take Cover' signal by whistles, delaying evacuation till they are satisfied that it can be carried out in reasonable safety.

## Christine Haig's story

Christine Haig didn't start her working life in an aircraft factory. She'd been working as a secretary for a stationery firm near her home in Washwood Heath when she turned eighteen in 1942. By that time, young unmarried women were being called up to work in some capacity for the war effort. 'You got a letter from the government and you had to do it,' she recalled. 'I was told I'd be working in an aircraft factory, but I had no idea at first what I was going to do. I'd just been promoted in my office job and I was earning £4 a week. At the factory, I got £7 a week – the women got £7 and the men got £14 a week. There were big blocks in the factory with hundreds working in each block. One section would be putting the metal skin onto the wings. It would be wheeled down on a trolley. Before we got them, the wings were up on gantries with four men working on them, riveting them. It was really noisy, what with all the riveting guns going on.'

Christine was teamed with another girl, working on the wings. Further down her production line, other girls would be working in pairs on smaller parts for the planes.

'Our work was on the curved edge of the wing that goes right to the tip. We had a metal strip to push inside the wing. The strip of metal was about 14 to 16 inches long. Men's hands are too big but us girls could get our hands in. We had to drill it and screw it for extra strength on the side of the leading edge. Then, when we'd finished and it was taken from us, it was wheeled back to another department so that they could fasten the wing onto the body of the plane.

'Sometimes we'd do twelve or fourteen in one day – and that was some going. It was really hard work getting the screws in if you'd never been used to it. But we were more or less left to it. We knew what we had to do once we got into the job and we just carried on. The wings kept coming down to us and we completed them.'

The girls worked from 7 a.m. until 6 p.m. during the week. Christine would leave home at 6 a.m. for a tram ride followed by a bus to the factory site. 'On Fridays, if they were short of planes, you were given an hour off and continued to work round the clock to 7 a.m. on a Saturday morning. We didn't work nights and there wasn't a lot of bombing during the day, though the place was bombed at night a couple of times. Two of my friends were killed at the factory, just the month before I started. There was a big brick shelter at the side of the factory but, to be honest, I don't think it would have been much good if they had bombed us.'

The factory site was very close to the Castle Bromwich aerodrome. Like Eileen Weston, Christine would sometimes see the completed planes being taken to the aerodrome. 'We'd watch them push them across the road; eight men could push one quite easily. And when they reached the aerodrome, the test pilots would be waiting there. Everyone used to cheer as they pushed them across. Facing the road were about a dozen RAF houses, so the pilots could be on tap all the time.'

At the time, Christine was saving up to get married to her fiancé, Frank. He worked in a different factory. 'We'd been courting since I was fourteen. I'd pay my mum £3 a week out of my wages, the rest I'd put in the bank. Frank wasn't called up but some of the younger men working in the factory were. Every so often you'd notice that one of the younger men you'd chat to would be missing because of the call-up. Then others would replace them and have to be taught how to do the work.'

Women workers in the factory were definitely a minority. But the general atmosphere was friendly. 'Some of the men working in the factory were my dad's age, so they looked after us. Yes, it was really hard work. But it was also enjoyable working there. You knew you were doing your bit for the war effort and that was what mattered.'

Christine finished at Castle Bromwich in March 1945, just before war officially ended. 'I was getting married and they were already cutting staff down. We helped build thousands of Spitfires at Castle Bromwich then but I'm not at all surprised that the Spitfire continues to fascinate people. It's a marvellous plane.'

In 2014, Christine met some of the surviving Castle Bromwich test pilots at a big reunion at the Birmingham Museum. 'One of them kissed my hand, thanked me for what I'd done. They were a different breed. Real gentlemen.'

## Miss Shilling's Orifice

At the Royal Aircraft Establishment in Farnborough, tests were carried out in 1940 on a captured Luftwaffe fighter plane, a Me 109, just before the Battle of Britain. These tests showed that the German fighter plane had a huge advantage over the early Mark I Spitfires and Hurricanes. It could go into a sudden dive without losing power because its engine, the Daimler-Benz DB 601, had fuel injection. This meant that in a dogfight, the German plane could escape quickly. Yet the British fighters could not chase the plane due to the carburettors in the Rolls-Royce Merlin engine, which suffered sudden fuel loss when the pilot put the nose down in a power dive; at that point the engine would temporarily cut out because of the effects of negative G flooding the carburettor with fuel.

In such a situation, the only thing a Spitfire or Hurricane pilot could do was a half roll or turn the plane on its back to restore the flow of fuel. This required a degree of skill – and it also wasted time. Yet at that point, making swift changes to the carburettors of the fighters was a complex task. Frustratingly, despite all the testing of the Spitfires and Hurricanes prior to production, it had not been understood that sudden dives would play such a big part in combat.

Throughout the Battles of France and Britain, pilots would return from sorties to complain about the sudden engine cut-out. Lives were being lost, too. How could the problem be solved without replacing the carburettors? Enter Miss Beatrice Shilling, a butcher's daughter from Waterlooville, Hampshire.

At just fourteen, 'Tilly' Shilling rode a Royal Enfield motorcycle, an unusual pastime for a young woman in the 1920s. An electrical engineering graduate at Manchester University in an era when women very rarely chose such an option (she was one of just two female students studying engineering), Tilly joined the Royal Aircraft Establishment at Farnborough in their engine department just before war broke out. And it was her clear thinking and inventiveness that came up with a simple, elegant solution to the engine cut-out problem.

Tilly devised a small metal disc with a hole in the middle – a flow-restrictor that could be fitted into the Merlin engine's carburettor. This would limit fuel flow and allow the engine to keep going in a dogfight dive. Officially, it was called the RAE restrictor. But after Tilly and her team had visited frontline RAF fighter bases to fit the restrictor in the winter of 1941, grateful pilots dubbed her invention 'Miss Tilly's Diaphragm' or 'The Tilly Orifice'. By March 1941, the Tilly restrictor had been installed throughout RAF Fighter Command and its inventor entered RAF folklore.

The Tilly orifice continued to be used as a temporary measure in the aircraft until a pressure carburettor was introduced in 1943. Shilling was awarded the OBE in 1948 and in subsequent years continued to indulge in her abiding passion for engines, racing both motorbikes and cars together with her husband, George Naylor, who also worked at the RAE. Tilly's work there continued in the supersonics division and the guided weapons section. When she eventually retired in 1969, she held a senior post in the mechanical engineering department.

Even after retirement, she continued working on a consultancy basis for the aero industry and in later life was often seen tearing around in her souped-up Triumph Dolomite Sprint. She died in November 1990, aged eighty-one – an inspirational woman remembered with much gratitude by those in the aviation world who owed her so much.

# CHAPTER 3

○

# In the Air

IT TOOK GREAT COURAGE, SKILL AND tenacity to fly the Spitfire in combat and the history of this great plane is full of moving and inspirational stories. In this chapter, Spitfire pilots from around the world recall enduring friendships and heart-warming reunions, near misses and Hollywood parties, and remember some of those who lost their lives. With their own important role to play in the Spitfire's success, the women of the WAAF and the pilots of the ATA look back at the often hazardous conditions they faced to ensure the planes were ready for flight.

## A Premonition

Flight Lieutenant John F. Wilkinson was born in Northampton in 1923 and joined the RAF in 1941. He spent four years flying Spitfires with 41 Squadron and shot down five enemy aircraft. 'Just like a bird – it was perhaps the one machine in that period most incredibly attuned to flight,' he recalled afterwards. In the later years of the war, 41 Squadron was assigned to high-altitude Lancaster bomber escort.

'The long-distance flights to the Ruhr district and other targets in Germany with a 90-gallon belly tank were exciting events, recurring often. We flew top cover for the bombers. We were flying anywhere up to 35,000 feet with no pressurized cabin and no heat, strapped in tight for three hours, sitting on a collapsed rubber dinghy with the consistency of concrete, and under it a parachute. It was hard to relate that to the comforts of home. Our oxygen was not a forced system but rather used a regulator that provided oxygen on demand in accord with the altitude.

'In summer, flying over 30,000 feet was all right but in winter, at temperatures of minus 100 degrees Fahrenheit or lower, it was very uncomfortable to say the least. We had electrically heated slippers in our flying boots, waistcoats and gloves. There wasn't room in the cockpit for the heavy wool-lined leather jackets and trousers that the bomber crews wore. We only wore those on the ground. I wore silk stockings (as many did), long woollen underwear, a wool sweater and wool battledress. My grandmother had knitted long stockings of heavily treated seamen's wool, without feet, to fit inside my flying boots and cover my legs and hips.

'On my hands first came thin chamois leather gloves; easier to remove if one got burned than electrically heated gloves. And, finally, big standard issue elbow high leather gauntlets. Then, of course, we wore the Mae West life preservers (an inflatable vest-like jacket) when flying over water, which meant every flight from England to the Continent, and sometimes even when just in proximity to the sea. In the pouch behind my head in the Mae West I carried a tin of water – necessary if downed over land or water.

'In the tunic of my battle dress there were two inside pockets, one on each side. In each one of those I carried a survival pack. The packs were curved plastic boxes shaped to fit against the chest. Each pack contained a week's supply of high-energy, highly compressed food, water purification pills and bag, fishing line and hook, sewing needle and thread. (In those days, trousers were held up with suspenders and buttons. If the buttons came off one would be rather conspicuous walking about holding up one's trousers!) Two of the less critical buttons could be removed and were designed such that when one was balanced on the spike in the middle of the other, they formed a compass with small dots to indicate north and south, vital if one was downed and able to evade capture. In addition, I carried a thin rubberized pouch that contained silk maps and a small hand knife. The maps were printed on silk so they would not make noise if one was caught and patted down.

'Our flying boots were wool lined. The shoe portion laced up and looked like an ordinary black walking shoe. The legging part of the boot contained a small knife that could be used to cut the stitching and remove it, making one less conspicuous during escape and evasion. I carried a large double-edged knife strapped to my shin with the handle above the legging part of my right boot. This was for easy access should I have to bail out and get caught up in a tree. I could then, with great care, cut myself loose. Along with all this, I carried my standard issue revolver and a pistol in a shoulder holster. Then, of course, there was the pilot's cloth helmet with built-in headphones and detachable oxygen mask with microphone. These got plugged in along with the electrically heated clothing after entering the cockpit. In the undesirable possibility of being downed, whether over enemy territory or rough seas, preparation can be the key to survival. I am thankful I never had occasion to use these emergency devices.'

After joining the RAF, Wilkinson had completed his early flight training in the US. In the first years of the war, there was an acute need to train new RAF pilots and the UK was not considered suitable given the combination of enemy action, high operational traffic at UK airfields and unpredictable weather, plus a shortage of training staff. As a consequence, air-training agreements were made with the United States, Canada and India. John Wilkinson had been sent to the Riddle McKay Aero College, Clewiston, in Florida. While there, he became great friends with another student pilot, Alfred George 'Bunny' Henriquez from Jamaica (then a British colony).

Bunny had volunteered to join the RAF Volunteer Reserve in 1941, receiving his initial training at Emmanuel College, Cambridge, and at Clewiston, Florida, after that. At twenty-two, he had married Essie Silvera and they had gone on to have two children – Kathleen, in 1939, and Richard two years later.

The friendship struck up by the two pilots was a strong one: back in England, the pair managed to keep up the friendship, even though both were flying in different parts of the country. In the spring of 1944, Bunny was flying Avro Lancaster bombers with 630 Squadron, based at East Kirby in Lincolnshire. Wilkinson was then flying with 41 Squadron on the south coast of England. It was there that Wilkinson developed 'a strong desire' to meet up with Bunny. Fortunately, he learned that there was a repaired Spitfire Mark IX that needed testing – and he was lucky enough to be given permission to test it and fly up to see Bunny.

'I had a good visit with him,' Wilkinson remembers. 'When I took off, he was standing by his Lancaster bomber.' Wilkinson circled once in his Spitfire as he made his farewell to Bunny. 'And as I did so, I somehow knew he would be killed.'

A few months later, on 17 August 1944, Flight Lieutenant Bunny Henriquez flew an Avro Lancaster on a night bombing raid of the Baltic port of Stettin in Poland. The plane was intercepted by a German night fighter, broke up in the air and crashed in pieces near Risznow, on the German–Polish border. At first, it was recorded that the plane had been missing in action without a trace. But later the Red Cross learned from the German authorities that the plane had crashed.

Wilkinson only discovered what had happened to his friend when Bunny's family wrote to him with the sad news. 'They told me his small daughter, Kathleen, had woken in the night screaming "Pray for Daddy!" Some time later, Wilkinson discovered that this had happened on the same night that Bunny was killed.

Disaster struck Bunny's family again, just three days after Bunny's wife, Essie, had received a telegram telling her that her husband was missing in action. On 20 August, one of the strongest hurricanes of the twentieth century hit Port Maria, on the north coast of Jamaica, where

Essie, her mother and children were living. As Bunny's son Richard, who became a successful architect, recounts, 'When the hurricane hit, large sections of the roof of their house were gone. It was a terrifying experience; the metal roofing was torn off. Crockery was blown out of the cupboards and crashed onto the floor. When the winds finally died down there were dead fish everywhere and hundreds of trees flattened.'

Essie was devastated, her husband lost, her home destroyed. Yet she had to carry on somehow. 'At the end of 1944, soon after it had been confirmed that Bunny was dead, Essie received a life-changing letter from Frank Henriquez, Bunny's first cousin. She already knew him well. Here she was, a young widow, her home in ruins, two small children to care for and here was someone who cared for her deeply, and appeared to be offering her a new life.' They married two years later and emigrated to Vancouver, Canada.

'My mother and Frank went on to have three children. Four of the family of five children remained in Canada, one went to live in the US. On 17 August 1994, I travelled to my father's grave in Poland.' Richard learned that the bodies of his father and the crew of seven men had initially been brought by horse-drawn cart from the crash site and buried in the churchyard at the village of Risznow. They were later transferred to the Old Garrison Military Cemetery at Poznań, Poland.

'Fifty years later, all that my mother could say was: "I was very young", when I asked her how she felt about his decision to leave us and go to war. If she harboured any resentment, she never expressed it,' says Richard. 'I have no recollection of him at all, while my sister Kathleen carries a dim image of being lifted out of, or put into a car by him, in the garage at our grandparents' home.

'There is no doubt that I grew up with a large hole in my life, a tangible, though, until recently, unrecognized sense of loss. A sense of loss expressed verbally for the first time on 17 August 1994 as I confronted my father's grave in Poland and said: "I missed you, Daddy, I missed you."

John Wilkinson died on 2 February 2017, aged ninety-four.

## Survival in the Balkans

Flying Officer Richard Day joined the RAF in 1940 and had a distinguished war career flying Spitfires and Hurricanes in England and across the Mediterranean with 253 (Hyderabad State) Squadron. In July 1944, he was posted to Termoli, on the Adriatic coast of Italy, part of the recently formed Balkan Air Force set up to assist Marshall Tito's pro-Communist Partisans in attacking long range targets in Albania, Yugoslavia and Greece, and provided increased supplies and tactical air support for the Partisans. Day's squadron was equipped with Spitfire Vs and later VIIIs and IXs.

In October 1944, Day was wounded by an intense burst of small-arms fire through the aircraft's cockpit canopy, but he quickly recovered and returned to operations the following month. Then, on 26 February 1945, while attacking a motor transport convoy in the area of

Bos-Novi in the former Yugoslavia (now known as Novi Grad in Bosnia and Herzegovina, on the border with Croatia) his Spitfire was hit in the glycol tank, again by small-arms fire. The attack took place in a valley and the Spitfire was hit when flying at virtually ground level.

Day pulled hard on the control column to climb as quickly as possible out of the valley. He tried to attain height at least 500 ft above the surrounding mountain peaks. But because the radiator temperature was now going 'off the clock' there remained only one thing to do – bail out. He called his Number Two, Warrant Officer Pete Blyth, disconnected his radio plug, jettisoned the hood, selected full forward on the aircraft trim, held back the control column against the force exerted by the trim tab and undid his cockpit straps.

As he shot out of the cockpit, one leg caught on the harness, but Day managed to kick himself free. Out he went. Away from the engine and the slipstream there followed a few seconds of absolute silence before he pulled the parachute ripcord. The canopy quickly opened and he gently dropped to earth, landing very quickly amongst the snow-covered mountains. Using his commando knife, he managed to cut shrouds from the canopy, intending to use them for cover, and to wrap around himself for warmth.

Then he started to make his way westward through the snowy terrain. He had been trained to handle appalling mountain conditions prior to his commencing ground attack operations over the area. In daylight hours he mostly hid in slits in the rocks, wrapped in the canopy, with snow for his front door. Only at night would he trudge forward as best he could. There always seemed to be sufficient light to make some progress. There was, he knew, a chance that he might encounter any one of the three main groups who were fighting in the area.

If he encountered a Partisan group, the communist-led Resistance to the Axis powers in German-occupied Yugoslavia, known as the People's Liberation Army, commanded by Marshall Tito, he knew he'd probably find safety and shelter, since the Tito group were largely considered to be safe and helpful. A second anti-German group, known as the Chetniks, a Serbo-Croatian nationalist movement, led by General Mihailović and his followers, might be friendly, but he couldn't be certain. The third group in the area were the German-trained Ustaše. They were to be avoided at all cost – Croatian nationalists who promoted genocide against Serbs, Jews and Romani people and had already slaughtered hundreds of thousands.

Day had a small supply of food with him: Horlicks tablets and chocolate. For water, he resorted to melting snow. He navigated by the stars, kept to the mountain area and stayed away from the valleys. After four days' trekking, he awoke one morning to find himself looking into the barrel of a Tommy gun held by a Partisan. One of Tito's group, thankfully. There were five men, none spoke English. Yet the word 'RAFF' seemed to mean something to them.

The airman travelled with the Partisans along the mountain tracks. At night, the group slept around a central fire in deserted stone shelters (shepherd's summertime huts). Soon they were joined by another group of about fifteen, including two female soldiers, all armed with rifles and sub-machine guns of the MP-40 type. Their food consisted of meatballs with garlic, rough bread and a thin soup with dumplings.

Day spent three days trekking with the Partisan group on foot and horseback, until they reached a British military mission (No. 37) where two British Army personnel, an officer and an NCO, were located in a house overlooking a disused airstrip. Their equipment included a radio set and they made a daily radio call to Bari, Italy at 6 p.m. Whilst Day was in their care, the Mission benefited from a supply airdrop, including a small flagon of rum, Nelson's Blood. At breakfast there was real spam and eggs, traded with locals in return for English or American cigarettes.

The Mission was not detected by German aircraft and after five days a message from Bari came through: a Dakota was on its way to pick Day up. On departing from the airstrip, there was a small satisfaction. Spitfires from his own Squadron, 253, were there to escort the Dakota back to base.

A week or so later, after interrogation and de-lousing, he was back on operational flying. In August 1945, Richard Day was awarded the Distinguished Flying Cross. Afterwards, he joined his father's flour milling and animal feeds business in Boston, Lincolnshire, married Margaret Hodder and had four children. He died in Boston, aged eighty-six, on 21 April 2010.

## A WAAF's Terrifying Experience

On the ground, Spitfires required great skill and special handling. Due to the big powerful engine, the plane was nose heavy. So prior to flight, when the pilot opened the throttle to check the magnetos, oil pressure, engine temperature, pneumatic systems, oxygen and other systems, it was necessary to have a ground crew member lay on the tail to keep the plane from nosing over. Early Spitfires needed one ground crew member, but later, more powerful Spitfires required up to four ground crew members to keep the plane steady.

Flight Lieutenant John F. Wilkinson recalled one memorable incident he witnessed early in the war. 'The pilot, with a WAAF [Women's Auxiliary Air Force] member lying on his tail, began running his pre-flight check without waiting for the WAAF to dismount, forgetting she was there.'

The Women's Auxiliary Air Force (WAAF) was the female auxiliary of the RAF during the Second World War. Formed in June 1939, initially the women's roles were driving, cooking and clerical work. However, as war progressed and more women joined, WAAF women's roles developed considerably and they became involved in mechanics, engineering and a number of more skilled roles, including interception of codes. In the early war years, they were frequently required to work with ground crews engaged in pre-flight checks, an essential list of tasks performed by pilots and crew before take-off. The purpose of these checks was to improve flight safety.

But these didn't always go to plan, as Wilkinson explained: 'He opened the throttle and took off. Once the throttle is opened, the force of the slipstream makes it very difficult to dismount. She remained, clinging to the tail for dear life. As he climbed away from the airfield, the pilot felt something was wrong, so he circled and then landed, with one terrified, but alive, WAAF on the tail. It's safe to say she never assisted a pilot again by laying on the tail.'

## An Unexpected Reunion

Flight Lieutenant Jimmy Taylor joined 16 Squadron in their Strategic Reconnaissance Wing in August 1944. His first mission was photographing Caen Airfield, flying Spitfire K954. 'Our job was long-distance reconnaissance, usually concerned with future advances of the Army, so that one of our jobs was to do mapping of the likely countryside that the Army would be fighting over after it had finished whatever they were doing at the moment. Our job was to photograph the countryside and enable them to improve the maps because the maps they had were generally out of date and not very accurate.

'We had plenty of pilots – twenty in the squadron – and about twenty-five aircraft. On a very good day of weather they'd all be airborne at the same time. But that autumn of 1944 the weather was pretty bad 90 per cent of the time and we sometimes didn't fly at all for five days because the weather just never opened up. It was raining but the cloud was very low. The cloud, in fact, was our biggest enemy, probably bigger than the Germans. We could hear the rotating disc of their radar aerial picking us up on our earphones as soon as we got airborne, but it didn't automatically mean we were going to get shot down or attacked. Even if we were in cloud we could be seen. But it's very difficult to send an aeroplane after you if you're flying in a cloud and, in our case, we liked flying in cloud. I preferred cloud where you were safe, rather than flying in the open where you could be pounced on.'

On Sunday 19 November 1944, Jimmy was flying a Spitfire Mark IX on a sortie from Melsbroek Airfield, Brussels, to take photos of airfields in the Rheine area of Germany, near a town called Rheine, not far from the Dutch border. The weather was fine, the best for a week. 'On 16 Squadron, we didn't have personal aircraft. When we reached the top of the list for the next mission we took the next plane that happened to have been made ready. That day was busy: all the aircraft were up except for one rather tired aeroplane. So I spun a coin with another pilot over who should take it and I got it. In fact, I'd flown it two or three times before and was quite happy with it.

'I was happily taking my photographs at 24,000 feet over three airfields at Rheine when all of a sudden there was an enormous bang. The engine coughed and spluttered. Smoke and flames came out of the exhausts. The flames stopped but the smoke became thicker and thicker, followed by black oil. The windscreen became covered and I could not see out. There was a long plume of black smoke behind me in the sky. I called up my base near Brussels on the radio and told them the news. They gave me a course to steer and a gliding speed of about 140 mph and told me to head back towards Brussels. Unfortunately, that day at 24,000 feet we had hundred-mile-an-hour winds blowing against me and I knew I was not going to make a great deal of progress gliding – and then flames started coming out of the exhaust and smoke began to come up into the cockpit. There was an 85-gallon petrol tank between the engine and the cockpit. I had visions of the flames getting near the petrol tank and the whole wretched thing exploding. Then the radio cut out – perhaps burned out or because I was too low to receive calls from a distance.

'I decided to bail out. I thought I'd do a very good bailout because I had plenty of time – I wasn't being shot at or anything, though I expected the Germans to be alert to the fact that there was a plane up there with a great trail of smoke behind it, so I had time to unplug my oxygen mask, put my maps in my flying boots and undo the straps holding me in my seat. I knew in my head what I was going to do: turn the Spitfire upside down and drop out. Which I did.

'But either I hit the tail or the aircraft turned and hit me because I felt a severe blow in my midriff. It knocked me out. Then I recovered consciousness. I was falling through space and I thought I was cut in half – I didn't think I had any legs left. Then a little voice said, "Pull the string, pull the string." I felt too ill to worry whether the parachute would work or not and I could see the parachute fluttering out between my legs. I felt a small sense of relief – and passed out again.

'When I came to, I found myself over a wide river or canal. I thought vaguely I might drown. I next saw a man riding a bike along a lane and thought it funny he could not see me. A green field rushed up towards me and I remembered the advice "Legs together, legs together!" as I hit the ground and rolled over. Somehow I staggered to my feet and found a wood. I sat there for a time and thought:

"This is stupid, the Germans will come and look for me and they're bound to look in the wood first of all." Then I saw a ditch going through an enormous field and thought, "If I get in that ditch in the middle of the field I'll be safe and I will see people coming towards me before they can see me." So I got in the ditch. It had a little bit of water in the bottom and I spent the rest of the day there. I saw soldiers with rifles on their backs on bicycles cycling through the lane, but nobody came near me.'

From that point on, Taylor made his way through the countryside on foot, deciding to go west for as long as possible, then hoping to strike south across the Rhine.

He was pretty sure he was in The Netherlands. The Battle of Arnhem had taken place a few weeks before but Taylor was not sure whether the 21st Army had reached the Rhine at some point. All he could think of was somehow getting back to Brussels.

'I had a date with a girl in Brussels on the Wednesday and I knew my best friend in the squadron would take her over if I was not there!' (Jimmy was right. Years after the war, the couple asked him to be godfather of their first child.)

Jimmy knew all too well he was in serious danger of being captured. He was also aware that a curfew was in place in both Germany and the Netherlands and that the countryside he was traversing was alive with Germans, who were occupying the Netherlands. Yet somehow he managed to keep going for nearly four days. On 24 November, Jimmy had passed a sign saying Doorn (in Utrecht, central Netherlands) when he realized he was in an area called *Kampfzone* (combat zone). Turning off the main road onto a side road, he decided to follow an old couple pushing a pram piled high with household possessions. But he was soon stopped by a passing German officer on a bike, with an MP-40 sub-machine gun around his neck, who asked him what he was doing. Initially, he let Jimmy go but then had second thoughts. The game was up. 'I said, "What do you want?" and he said, "*Komm mit mir*," and joggled the gun. The end of freedom!'

Afterwards, Jimmy was held in a prison camp with paratroopers captured at Arnhem and then taken to an interrogation centre in Frankfurt. Finally, in May 1945, he arrived at Stalag Luft 1 POW Camp for Allied airmen, near Barth on the Baltic. Liberated by the Russians on 1 May, two weeks later Jimmy was flown back to freedom in England. 'Fortunately we had a brilliant commanding officer at 16, Squadron Leader Tony Davis (DFC). We were all rather individuals and he held us together because we had an enormous respect for him: he took all the most difficult tasks and wouldn't tell anyone, just disappear. We only knew he'd been somewhere when he came back and occasionally we'd discover he'd taken a difficult target. He also knew when to pile us into his car and take us into a café in France or Belgium – he knew when we needed that sort of relaxation.

'When I was missing, because I'd radioed up they knew I was okay and they knew I was going to bail out. [Davis] flew back and went to my parents' house and spent time with them. He told them the chances of me being alive were pretty good – that there was a 50/50 chance I'd bailed out successfully and been captured, and would be back at the end of the war. From that point of view he was brilliant and my parents very much admired him for doing this. He did the same for other people's parents, too, if he could.'

After a period instructing on Harvards at RAF Upavon, Jimmy left the RAF in June 1946. Cambridge University followed, then a long career teaching history, including a spell in Baghdad with the British Council. Yet the story of that last Spitfire flight and the bailout in 1944 was due to impact on Jimmy's life in another way that he could never have imagined.

In March 1990, Hennie Noordhuis, an archivist from a small town in eastern Holland called Borne, placed an advertisement in the journal of the RAF Association, asking after the whereabouts of Flight Lieutenant James Strickland Taylor, who had bailed out of Spitfire PL957 on 19 November 1944 and been taken prisoner. It was Jimmy's plane. At the time, Jimmy was on a trip to RAF Laarbruck in Germany to celebrate 16 Squadron's seventy-fifth anniversary. He was handed the clipping from the magazine. Intrigued, he contacted Hennie Noordhuis. It turned out that Jimmy's flying helmet and goggles had been picked up by local Dutchmen when he'd landed and stumbled off. For decades, the identity of the pilot had remained untraceable until some dogged detective work by Noordhuis revealed the name of the pilot.

Later, in a phone call with Noordhuis, Jimmy heard what had happened after he'd gone on the run. It was shattering news. 'When the Germans could not find the pilot of the crashed Spitfire, they had taken six hostages at random from the people of the scattered hamlet of 't Hesseler, where I'd come down.'

'On 25 November, the day I had been captured seventy miles away, they had shot three of the hostages in a field close to the landing place, watched at a distance by friends and relatives. During the war, over seven hundred Allied and German planes had crashed in this small area and many aircrew were made prisoners. At the same time, the Dutch Resistance was very active blowing up bridges and canal locks, sabotaging production, calling strikes in factories. The Germans were particularly antagonistic to the Resistance. So they had accused them of hiding me. The executions were intended as a reprisal and a deterrent.'

In 1991, Jimmy and his wife Margaret made the first of many visits to Borne and 't Hesseler in the Netherlands to meet with Noordhuis and his family and friends to remember the innocent men whose lives were tragically lost.

On one such trip in April 1995, much to his amazement, Jimmy was taken to the crash site and there he was reunited with the collected remains of his Spitfire, 'more than fifty years after I'd turned the burning machine upside down and dropped out of it.

'We drove to Hennie Egberink's contractor's yard. Hennie had been in the Resistance during the war and was a member of the liberation committee of Borne from 1945 to 1995. He welcomed us and there, on the ground, was one large mass of identifiable metal and innumerable unrecognizable scraps of all different kinds of materials that made up the once-familiar shape of the photo-reconnaissance Spit.

'Our Spit IXs were painted a very distinctive sky-blue and I was fortunate in picking out half a dozen fragments with dull, but nevertheless definite blue patches of paint on them and these I hoarded carefully in a plastic bag. Seeing the remains of the plane after its dramatic recovery and meeting the people who had witnessed its descent – and mine – all this left little room for sleep. My head was alive with memories of 19 November 1944, my poorly executed bailout, my somewhat erratic route over the Rhine over five days, my bitter frustration at being taken prisoner followed by the tragedy of the hostages caught up in the Germans' brutal and senseless reprisals. I would return to the remains of my beautiful Spitfire L957 three times, but after that first visit I did not sleep much that night.'

Flight Lieutenant Harold James 'Jimmy' Strickland Taylor died in December 2016, aged ninety-four.

## Eager for the Air

The ATA's (Air Transport Auxiliary) motto summed it up: *Aetheris Avidi* – Eager for the Air. Without the services of the ATA, a civilian organization, delivering the brand new Spitfires and all the other new aircraft urgently needed by the RAF and the Fleet Air Arm during the Second World War, Britain's history might have been quite different.

The ATA was founded at the outbreak of the Second World War to provide a crucial backup auxiliary service to the RAF and the Royal Navy, taking over from service pilots in order to ferry brand new planes across the country from factory to airfield, as well as collecting and returning damaged planes between maintenance units and frontline squadrons. Essentially, the ATA's remit was to ensure that all new or repaired RAF aircraft were flown precisely where they needed to be – a hugely complex exercise in logistics and planning.

Sometimes jokingly referred to as 'Ancient and Tattered Airmen' many of the ATA's earlier recruits were either Great War veterans too old for combat or those whose health or injury problems prevented them from flying for the RAF. Those working for the organization totalled just over 4,000, including 2,786 ground staff and admin workers, plus 1,245 pilots and engineers from twenty-five different countries. At one point, the ATA was known as 'the Foreign Legion of the air' because so many different countries were represented. By the end of the war the ATA had safely ferried 300,000 plus aircraft of 147 different types of planes from light trainers to four-engine bombers, including brand new Spitfires.

Yet what made the ATA quite unique in aviation was that 168 out of 1,245 of the pilots and flight engineers who ferried and delivered Spitfires, Hurricanes, Barracudas, and many others across the UK to the RAF, were women from all over the world: Chile, Poland, the US, New Zealand, South Africa and many other countries. This was the first time in the history of British aviation that wartime fighter planes and bombers had women seated at the controls.

In a sense, ATA pilots were test pilots, often required to collect a brand new plane that had never been flown before direct from the production line. As aircraft production increased through the war years, frequently the ferry pilots were required to deliver a type of new plane they had never even seen before, using a handbook called *Ferry Pilots Notes*, as guidance through the hazards. This was dangerous work.

Until D-Day, ferry pilots flew around the UK only, but the hazards existed: they flew unarmed, usually without radio, and often without fully functional navigational instruments. They had to deal with barrage balloons (these were set up in the air across the country in order to deter enemy bombers. They were 66 feet long and 30 feet high when inflated) and the unpredictability of the British weather – life threatening if flying into heavy cloud, and, in the early years of the war, extremely uncomfortable if flying in open-topped cockpits. (One-hundred and seventy-three ATA ferry pilots lost their lives during the war, mostly due to bad weather, including the pioneering aviator Amy Johnson.) Moreover, if they were unlucky, they could encounter a German fighter plane. Yet such was the non-stop nature of their task, many ATA pilots had flown hundreds of Spitfires, as well as other types of planes, by the time the war ended.

### First Officer Ray Roberts

Ray Roberts joined the RAF in December 1938 as a trainee pilot and had already completed his first solo flight. But he had an unlucky incident when his training plane, a Miles Master, caught fire and he had to bail out. Ray's parachute didn't open fully and his ankles were damaged, leaving him unable to fly fighter or bomber planes for the RAF. Yet he was not in the least deterred by the incident. He wanted to keep flying. 'After the accident, my wife Lily came to the hospital and said: "Well, if you're going back to flying, Ray, I'm going to be the one to pack your parachute for you in future!"'

Little did she know that very soon she'd be packing more

than just one parachute. For when a friend told Ray that the ATA were urgently seeking ferry pilots, Ray was quick to apply. 'My leg hadn't mended properly but I got in. By the end of the war I was able to fly jet fighters,' he recalled.

Lily joined the ATA, too. For a two-year period, the couple were even based at the same ferry pool in Whitchurch, near Bristol. And as a Safety Officer, one of Lily's jobs was packing parachutes. 'Sometimes we'd even wind up flying on the same delivery plane together – she'd be packing parachutes for two different stations, mine and another one within 40 miles, so she'd be getting on the plane, loading it up with parachutes to bring back,' explained Ray.

Roberts' ATA log book records some 147 Spitfire deliveries from the time he joined in October 1940 until leaving the ATA in November 1945. He ferried and delivered planes across the UK until just after D-Day and the Normandy Landings, when Roberts and other male ATA pilots were also needed to make regular delivery flights to the Continent. They ferried passengers, too, including freed Allied POWs, war orphans, medical teams and wounded servicemen. (In the last days of the war, a few ATA women pilots were cleared to fly in and out of Europe, too.)

On Ray's second ever Spitfire delivery, he was coming into land when he realized the needle had fallen off the air speed indicator. 'Normally you brought them in at 85 mph, but I managed to land quite safely without the air speed indicator. I probably brought it in at 90 mph,' he recalled.

Ray recalled another truly memorable Spitfire delivery incident in September 1942, which proved to be the cause of much mirth. Ray was ferrying a Spitfire Mark V from

Hawarden, on the England/Wales border, to Yeovilton in Somerset. All went well until he came into land – and encountered an unknown hidden hazard.

'I was delivering a damaged Spitfire for repair at Yeovilton, but during landing the flaps and brakes suddenly failed, so I had to land on the grass and the plane hit a little heap of asphalt. No one knew it was there. I was probably doing 90 mph so the plane was upended onto its nose, standing upright. It was amazing.'

The sight of Ray climbing out of the upended Spitfire by sliding down the nose was vastly amusing to the ground crew who rushed to photograph the upended Spit. 'One of the crew described the ending to the crash: "A little fat figure went sliding down – and ran off." Afterwards we all had a good laugh about that – you tended to laugh about anything and everything in the war. But that was the story of the end of my twenty-second Spitfire flight – and I wasn't even fat!'

After war ended, Ray went back into the RAF, flying Tiger Moths and Austers until he left in 1956 to run his own business as a turf accountant, taking and paying off bets on sporting events. In 1968 he became a gliding instructor for 618 Squadron and taught RAF cadets, finally retiring in 1970.

His wife Lily died in November 2005, aged ninety-one. Yet like so many other people, Ray's wartime relationship with the Spitfire never quite ended. In 2016, when he reached his 100th birthday, his family gifted him a twin-seater Spitfire flight from Biggin Hill and in February 2017, he was invited as a special guest to participate in the Biggin Hill centenary celebrations with a second flight in a Spitfire. On his 100th birthday flight, he joyfully navigated the Spitfire for ten minutes. 'You never forget it,' he said afterwards. 'It's such a nice, smooth fighter.'

## ACCIDENT REPORT

Here's the accident report of what happened to the Mark V R7207 on 13 September 1942:

Aircraft landed with flaps up, overshot aerodrome and was damaged by striking a heap of road material.

Cause: Jamming of the starboard flap on the trailing edge of the main plane.

Pilot not held responsible for this accident. Attention of the Chief Engineer is called to this accident.

### The Women of the ATA

There were just eight female pilots flying for the ATA in January 1940, working out of a muddy base in Hatfield, near London, flying in open cockpit training planes (de Havilland Tiger Moths) in harsh, wintry conditions. That they were permitted to fly for the ATA at all was largely due to the determination and efforts of one woman, the redoubtable Pauline Gower, an MP's daughter and experienced commercial pilot who had lobbied furiously, against considerable resistance, for women pilots to be given the opportunity to fly during wartime.

The RAF had refused to consider female pilots. But in 1939, Gower's energy and commitment were rewarded when she was appointed to head up a women's section of the ATA. By September 1941, the numbers of female ATA pilots had grown to fifty. By then, the women pilots had been cleared to ferry operational aircraft: first, the Hurricane, then the Spitfire.

All-women ATA ferry pools were also set up at Hamble, near Southampton, close to the Vickers Supermarine Spitfire factory and in the Midlands at Cosford, near Birmingham, close to the Castle Bromwich Spitfire factory. This enabled the women pilots to make shorter ferry trips to and from the factories, enabling more aircraft to be ferried each day. They'd work to a rigorous schedule: thirteen successive days on, followed by two days off.

Lettice Curtis, who died in July 2014 at the age of ninety-nine, was one of the ATA's most celebrated female pilots, and one of the first women to qualify to fly heavy bombers for the ATA. She wrote about her time with the ATA in her book, *The Forgotten Pilots*. Writing about the Spitfire, she said: 'I never heard of anyone who did not enjoy flying it. It had a personality uniquely its own … To sit in the cockpit of a Spit, barely wider than one's shoulders … was a poetry of its own.'

Other female ATA pilots also retained powerful memories of the Spitfire. First Officer Mary Ellis delivered 400 Spitfires to 210 airfields and flew 76 different types of plane for the ATA from 1941 to 1945. In 2017, she also celebrated her 100th birthday. 'I'd already flown Hurricanes when I turned up to work one morning and learned I'd be ferrying a Spitfire from South Marston, near Swindon, to RAF Lyneham, my first ever Spitfire delivery. Then, once I'd delivered the first Spit, I'd be picked up by a taxi plane to take me back to South Marston, where I'd be flying the second Spitfire to the RAF at Little Rissington. On the very same day.' Mary had never been close to a Spitfire before so she was very anxious to do the right thing. 'This was a fast fighter plane. I'd better be good.'

Just as she was getting in, an engineer helpfully took her parachute and put it in. '"Hope you enjoy your flight. How many have you flown?" he enquired. He was horrified, poor man, when I explained it was my first Spitfire. A group of male engineers just stood there, watching me, wanting to see what would happen as I taxied out to the take-off point. I'm sure my little heart was beating very fast but … I was off! And somehow I managed an excellent take-off; once I was in the air I did a few manoeuvres to make sure I knew what I was doing. And then I set off for my thirty-minute flight. Thankfully, it was a very nice day. The Spit handled beautifully. It was thrilling.

'But, of course, there was the landing. There were no aids, you just went round the aerodrome and looked for a space between whatever else was flying and took your turn to land. I made a perfect landing. All my anxiety disappeared completely.' And the men who watched her take-off? 'I think they were horrified that this little fair-haired, young girl was flying a very valuable war machine twice in one day. But they seemed very happy when I got back to ferry the second one. One guy even gave me some of his sweet coupons as a reward.'

Molly Rose came from an aviation family, Marshalls of Cambridge, and had started to learn to fly at age sixteen. She was already working at Marshalls as a ground engineer, the company's first female engineering trainee, when war broke out, working long hours to repair Tiger Moths and other aircraft needing repair, cycling home at night in the blackout.

Newly married, when her husband Bernard was posted overseas in September 1940 she received a letter from the ATA inviting her to join the organization as a pilot. 'I was number ninety-eight on their list of females with pilots' licenses,' explained Molly. 'I knew they had women ferrying planes and I also had no idea how long I'd be parted from Bernard. A change, I reasoned, would be a very good idea.' After training, Molly was sent to the all-women ferry pool at Hamble. 'There was a pool of about thirty women pilots from all over the world: a real League of Nations. There was also a big age difference in the group. One woman, Lois Butler, was already a grandmother.'

The ATA women pilots had to have their uniforms specially fitted for them at Austin Reed in London. 'It was such a smart uniform; navy blue jacket, blue shirt, navy tie. The uniforms were really livery, you were meant to hand them in. I was a Third Officer – one gold bar on my epaulette. I was so proud of that.' (Molly would eventually be promoted to First Officer.)

When she finally left the ATA in May 1945, Molly had flown thirty-six different types of planes and delivered 486 aircraft, including 273 Spitfires. Yet of all the types of planes she ferried, the Spitfire was her clear favourite. 'Flying it was rather like putting on an overcoat: you fitted. It was a woman's plane; you could dance with the Spitfire.'

Nonetheless, there was one Spitfire incident that stood out in her memory. She was delivering a Spitfire from the Eastleigh factory, near Southampton, when the weather changed. 'I was ferrying it north and the weather was slightly dodgy. It seemed to be the sort of cloud you could get under or over. I was going over the Cotswolds. You didn't know what the ground was underneath you. Suddenly I was in bad cloud. I tried going under it; and came face to face with one of the Cotswold Hills. Fortunately for me, I had just enough power to pull the nose back and gain height fast. I just got over the hill. And I do mean "just". Thank God for power. That incident in the Spitfire made me very respectful of weather.' Molly Rose died in October 2016, aged ninety-five.

Margaret Frost was a parson's daughter from Sussex who became obsessed with flying as a child. Aged eleven, she would save up her pocket money just to be able to pay for the briefest of joyrides when the flying circuses set up locally. She applied to join the ATA just after war broke out because they'd asked for anyone with a pilot's licence to contact them. Yet because she'd only just started to fly, she was turned down.

She joined the WRNS (Women's Royal Navy Service) and was working as a 'plotter', plotting the paths of ships in and out of their harbours, when the ATA wrote to her again – by 1942 they urgently needed more ferry pilots. At her interview with the Chief Flying Instructor she was told she was too short, the height requirement was 5 ft 4 in

(1.62 cm) and Margaret was just under 5 ft 3 in. 'All my hopes of flying were dashed,' she recalled.

Then, to her surprise, the interviewer told her to sit down. He said he would discuss her application with the head of the ATA's women's section, Pauline Gower, and after that they would let Margaret know. '"Try and grow a little", was his parting shot,' recalled Margaret.

She was in. Margaret started with the ATA in November 1942 and went on to fly twenty-five different types of planes as a Third Officer until she finished flying for the ATA in September 1945.

She never forgot one of her last ever Spitfire deliveries to a depot in Scotland. 'On our chits for each delivery we made there was a section where you wrote down any comments you might have. This particular Spitfire had belonged to the Fleet Air Arm. I had to collect it for the last time ever from Henstridge, near Dorset. They were very upset to hand it over. We all knew she was going to be broken up. So I decided to express my feelings in words. I wrote on my chit: "THIS IS A BEAUTIFUL AEROPLANE AND SHOULD NOT BE BROKEN UP". The war was over. And everything was now quite different.' After 1950, Margaret worked for the MOD for twenty-five years. She retired in the mid-1970s and went to live in Wales. She died in August 2014, aged ninety-four.

Not long after war ended, Lord Beaverbrook, who had been Minister of Aircraft Production from 1940 to 1941 (see p. 22) paid generous tribute to the ATA's work: 'Without the ATA the days and nights of the Battle of Britain would have been conducted under conditions quite different from the actual events. They carried out the delivery of the aircraft from the factories to the RAF, thus relieving countless numbers of RAF pilots for duty in the battle.

'Just as the Battle of Britain is the accomplishment and achievement of the RAF, likewise it can be declared that the ATA sustained and supported them in the battle. They were soldiers fighting in the struggle just as completely as if they had been engaged on the battlefront.'

Despite the ATA's acknowledged role in helping win the war, many decades would pass before their largely unknown contribution to the war effort finally received a formal acknowledgement in the form of a medal, presented in 2008 to surviving ATA veterans by the then prime minister, Gordon Brown.

Aviation today, of course, bears little similarity to those perilous wartime deliveries when every single Spitfire delivery or repair from factory to RAF airfield was crucial to the country's very existence. Regulation and technology have combined to make a short plane trip a normal, everyday event. Yet even now, the idea of flying six different types of plane, including fighters and bombers, in a single day is still quite extraordinary. Let alone the idea of young women taking Spitfires up into the skies as mere part and parcel of a good day's work.

## AN UNUSUAL SIGHT

It was at RAF Millom in Cumberland in 1942 when Flight Mechanic Edgar Featherstone first saw a female ATA pilot. He'd been working there since 1941. 'I was on crew duty when I saw my first and only Second World War female pilot. She was at the controls of a Spitfire. Initially, I didn't know the gender of the pilot as I marshalled the aircraft into the allotted space near the control tower, placed the chocks in front of and behind the wheels and then made to climb on the wing to see if I could be of any help with straps, etc.' Edgar saw the pilot's helmet come off, before giving a brief shake of the head. 'And then the blonde hair came streaming out in the breeze!'

Edgar recalled that he was 'very impressed' with everything that happened after that, including the swarm of young officers who seemed to come from every corner of the airfield to view this ATA phenomenon. 'Where had they been hiding?' As a mere mechanic, Edgar stood there, awestruck. 'I was right out of the scene, of course, but I would dearly liked to have been very much part of it. I'd seen ATA pilot Amy Johnson of Hull before the war when she was being honoured after her intrepid flight to Australia.' But this was quite different. And he would never ever forget it.

## Movie Stars

Wing Commander Peter Ian Howard-Williams began his RAF career as a fighter pilot when he was twenty years old after completing his training at RAF Cranwell in March 1940. He joined 19 Squadron at RAF Duxford the same month and served with them throughout the Battle of Britain, flying Spitfires. From April 1941 to April 1942 he flew with 118 Squadron, RAF Ibsley, Hampshire, making frequent sorties across the Channel. 'Life in a fighter squadron was summed up very well by someone who said that a day consisted of twenty-three hours fifty minutes of boredom and ten minutes of sheer terror,' he wrote afterwards.

Yet the boredom and the terror were unexpectedly alleviated by an extraordinary event that took place at RAF Ibsley in the summer of 1941. A number of the fighter pilots found themselves appearing in a Hollywood film that year, *The First of the Few*, which told the story of the development of the Spitfire by R. J. Mitchell and his courage in continuing to work on its design, despite his illness.

Exteriors were to be shot at various locations including RAF Ibsley (portraying a fictional airfield in the south-east of England called 'Seafield') and a small number of veteran Battle of Britain pilots, more or less playing themselves, would be filmed in between combat operations. The contrast couldn't have been more stark: the life or death battle in the wartime skies against the glamour of a big Hollywood film crew. Its lead actors were Leslie Howard, who was also the producer and director, and David Niven, who had been given leave from the Army to star in the film as Squadron Leader Geoffrey Crisp, a fictional character reputed to be an amalgam of test pilots 'Mutt' Summers and Jeffrey Quill.

Howard-Williams remembered it all so well: 'Suddenly our lives were dramatically changed. A complete film unit was set up outside my dispersal. John Robson, the other Flight Commander in 118 Squadron, and I were chosen for two of the leading Spitfire pilot parts and it wasn't long before we were rehearsing scenes for the film.

'On 30th September, I flew a shipping reconnaissance patrol along the French coast and noted two medium-sized ships, probably flak ships [ships heavily armed with anti-aircraft weapons] ten miles north of Cherbourg. As soon as I had got back, a strike was laid on, with four Hurricanes and three other aircraft from 118 Squadron. We attacked the two flak ships, which were still in the same position.

'We did considerable damage and one ship sank. Unfortunately, my Number Two, Geoffrey Painting, was shot down. He was only seventeen and was a fully operational fighter pilot. John Robson had been badly shot up and had difficulty landing safely. The de-briefing was an introduction to the film people to our way of life.

'The next day I flew to Duxford to escort a captured Heinkel 111 to Ibsley for the use of the film company. It had German markings and for the next few weeks it flew around the area and nobody reported it or took any notice of it.

'The film unit stayed at the Kings Arms Hotel in Christchurch and some excellent parties were held while they were there. We had, on the Station, the dance band from one of the London nightclubs working in the Orderly Room. Also three top comedians in Station HQ, so we always had the basis for a party. David Niven had recently married the lovely Primula Rollo, and came in for some stick if it seemed they had sneaked off to bed early!

'The film continued to be made between offensive and defensive patrols, bomber escorts and convoy patrol duty. We would sometimes be in the middle of a scene when the alarm would go and Leslie Howard would suddenly find himself without any actors! We scrambled to meet the incoming raid. We returned an hour or so later, having perhaps destroyed some enemy aircraft, attacked some shipping, or as sometimes happened the Germans had turned round, mid-channel, and gone home. If some of the actors did not return it was necessary to shoot some of the scenes again with someone else.

'Life seemed a little dull when the film unit left after one tremendous party at the Kings Arms. As winter approached, flying was often restricted by bad weather and we settled down to normal squadron routine. Then one day, John Robson and I were called to the orderly room and told that we had been detached for a week. This was not received with any great enthusiasm until the Squadron Adjutant said that our detachment was to Denham Film Studios to continue working on *The First of the Few*. Orders had come from HQ Fighter Command.

'We packed our suitcases, were given railway warrants and caught the train to London where we booked into a cheap hotel. After a quick wash we went to meet Leslie Howard's publicity manager. He at once apologized profusely because he couldn't get us into the Dorchester Hotel but had got us each a suite at the Savoy Hotel and would that be alright? With the help of a large brandy each we recovered sufficiently to explain that it was fine and that we had left our luggage at the station. We dashed back to our hotel, collected our luggage, paid the bill for one night and treated ourselves to a taxi to the Savoy. Leslie Howard was there to greet us, and very firmly told us both that he had made arrangements with the manager of the hotel, who had notified all the staff, that we were to sign for everything and on no account were we to pay for anything. He had recently sold the film *Pimpernel Smith* for a lot of money in America. 'That night we managed to round up twenty-eight for dinner and the only money I spent in the hotel was when I was in the bar one day with Leslie Howard and bought him a drink.

'The publicity manager came with us to various nightclubs, and we were often also accompanied by Leslie, David and his wife. David was a really first-class bird puller and was never allowed to leave until we had a table of pretty girls. After two or three days of monumental wining and dining with equally monumental hangovers to follow, there was a request for us to do some work and cars would be outside the Savoy at 7.30 the next morning to take us to the film studios. We were on the way to Denham by 7.45 and on our arrival found Leslie and David ready to start work. All went well and at the end of the day we were told we would be wanted for at least another day.

'Next day, we started work even earlier, and by mid-morning we were able to relax. My mother arrived to watch the filming and Leslie stopped everything until she was comfortably seated and with a good view of the proceedings. For five minutes he made her feel she was the most important person in the whole studio. There was only one word for it – charm – of which Leslie had plenty!

'Back to Ibsley, perhaps a little jaded, but with some good stories to tell the other pilots. David had a habit of reaching up for the overhead microphone, tell a funny story and reduce the whole set to laughter.'

Wing Commander Howard-Williams retired from the RAF in 1958. After retirement, he moved to Spain in 1979, returning to England in 1991. He died, aged seventy-three, in March 1993. In a letter written in October 1989, he recalled that brief appearance in the movie.

'I watched *The First of the Few* on TV recently and managed to video it. If you see it, I was one of the pilots who land early on and argue about who has shot down a Dornier. Then later sit down outside dispersal with David Niven saying one or two rather inane remarks! In the last part, I have a few close-ups in the cockpit.'

## Respect for the Enemy

It would have been a poignant sight, that spring of 1940. A fair-haired young English RAF pilot quietly praying in a half empty church in the medieval town of Bar-le-Duc, near Verdun in north-eastern France.

It was the time of the Phoney War, lasting from 3 September 1939 until 10 May 1940, when Germany invaded France and the Low Countries, a coastal region of Western Europe consisting of the Netherlands, Belgium and the low-lying area of the Rhine. The young man, Paul Richey, was already a veteran of aerial combat at twenty-four, and an extraordinary hero. He had shot down six German planes in a series of Number 1 Squadron patrols in the initial campaign in Northern France between March to May 1940, returning to his squadron base at Vassincourt, north-eastern France in his Hawker Hurricane each time. On 11 May, he was shot down – he managed to bail out but suffered concussion. Yet he returned to operational flying as soon as possible.

Richey flew his last patrol of the Phoney War on 19 May after downing his third He 111, hit by a burst of fire from a bomber's rear gunner. He managed to crash land in a field near Amiens with a serious bullet wound to the neck. He spent a month recovering in a Paris hospital, only to return to England to discover he'd been awarded a DFC (Distinguished Flying Cross, a military decoration awarded to RAF personnel for acts of courage, valour or devotion to duty while flying operations against the enemy).

So why was he praying that day in France? As he was to reveal the following year, in a book he wrote chronicling his months as a fighter pilot in the Battle of France, as it came to be known later, he was a religious man who had great respect and admiration for the courage of others. Even the enemy. The book, called *Fighter Pilot*, gave a detailed insight into the world of those who flew the early Hurricanes, written while Richey was recuperating from his bullet wound. It was published to great acclaim in 1941 and went on to become a bestseller (it is still in print today), the first ever account of aerial combat written by an RAF fighter pilot.

Although Richey admitted that he'd received 'a savage thrill' when shooting down German planes, he wrote of the German and British fighter pilot's mutual respect, too. Every time he knew he'd downed another pilot in battle, he felt compelled to find a local church and pray for them. 'My father was a Catholic and this was very important to him throughout his life,' explained his son, Simon. 'After a battle where he may have been responsible for a death he would find a local church and say a prayer for the dead man and his family. If he couldn't find a church that was open, he'd just kneel outside and say his prayers.'

Richey's RAF wartime career continued after the publication of his book. In the spring of 1941, he was finally fit enough to return to operational flying with 609 Squadron at Biggin Hill, where he would spend four months and complete fifty-three missions across the Channel. His Commander there was his lifetime friend, Michael 'Micky' Robinson, DFC, DSO. For Richey, the return to operational flying meant he'd now be flying Spitfires. He was not familiar with the Spitfire, so he was somewhat apprehensive about the change when he first arrived at Biggin Hill. It was Micky Robinson who provided reassurance.

'The Bishop (Flying Officer John Bisdee) took me up to the aerodrome in his little grey Austin to show me over the controls of a Spitfire,' Richey recalled of that time.

'Having been a Hurricane pilot for two years, I knew little about the Spitfire and had seldom even seen one. I also had the Hurricane pilot's conversion: I never hoped to fly a better fighter. This was perhaps understandable, for although an older machine than the Spitfire, the Hurricane had been well tried in peacetime. It had done magnificently in the Battles of France and Britain and had shot down far more enemy aircraft than the Spitfire. My own battles had been fought in the Hurricane, I had every confidence in it and I was thoroughly at home in one and "as one piece". I therefore approached my first Spitfire with a certain amount of distaste. I had seen them flying and admitted I had seen few prettier aircraft. But on the ground, to my biased eye, the Spitfire looked knock-kneed, flimsy and rather silly. It lacked the robust strength of my beloved Hurry. I had to admire its superior lines in flight. Then, she really did look a thoroughbred.

'As we walked over to get my flying helmet from the dispersal hut, the Bish gave me one or two tips regarding boost, pressure, speeds for lowering undercarriage and flaps, trimming for take-off, starting up and so on. Then, once seated in the cockpit, I buckled on my parachute harness and fighting harness, closed the small side door, started up, ran the engine up, waved the chocks and airmen away and taxied out to the downwind end of the runway in use. I flew three circuits and landings and some mild aerobatics, none of which I enjoyed. I found the elevators too sensitive, the ailerons too stiff, the nose too long and too high, the cockpit cramped and the vision restricted.

'The only thing I liked was the layout of the cockpit. The aeroplane flew all right. But the thought of fighting in it I relished not at all!

'I taxied in, feeling worried and disappointed, wondering whether it was the plane or me that was wrong. Micky was there to meet me. "How'd you like it?" he asked with a smile. "Not much," I said glumly. "Don't worry, old boy," he said, "I felt exactly the same after I'd come off Hurricanes, but after I'd done about twenty hours I wouldn't change it for anything. You'll see."'

Many years later, Paul reflected on the Spitfire and his own experience flying it, saying: 'Every aeroplane is a compromise between what the designer wants out of it and the operational needs. Some have good climb at the expense of something else, strength probably, because they have to make it light and have some manoeuvrability at the expense of speed, because it won't manoeuvre well if it's a very fast plane.

'The Spit was a good compromise: it had its faults like all aeroplanes and it had very sensitive elevators. However, the ailerons were very soggy. In some aircraft you could whip very quickly into a turn but in the others you couldn't. But the Spitfire made up for it in many other ways.'

'Later in 1941, Paul Richey was posted to Fighter Command, before being posted back to 609 Squadron, Duxford, as its Commanding Officer in June 1942. But personal tragedy was never very far away. In April 1942, 'Micky' Robinson, his close school friend and brother-in-law (Richey had married Robinson's sister Teresa in the winter of 1939) failed to return from a sweep and his Spitfire was reported lost over the Channel. He was just twenty-four.

Following postings as Wing Commander to the Far East

and India, Richey, who had suffered severe sinusitis at one stage, was invalided home in February 1944. After some time in hospital, he took up a post in SHAEF (Supreme Headquarters Allied Expeditionary Force), before ending the war at HQ, RAF 2nd Tactical Air Force. For a short period postwar, he worked for the *Daily Express* as air correspondent then later worked for BP. He was awarded the DFC and bar as well as the DSO (Distinguished Service Order). The DSO was awarded for distinguished service by officers of the Armed Forces in wartime, typically in combat. 'Bar' means that the medal has been won again – a bar is awarded rather than a second medal for the same honour. Richey was also awarded the Belgian and French Croix de Guerre. He died in 1989, aged seventy-two.

'Like a lot of fighter pilots who survived, what they'd lived through was such a profound experience that the war was never terribly far away,' said Simon Richey. 'My parents divorced just after the war. We saw my father frequently as he lived near us, but I was brought up by my mother. So as I grew up, the story of my father's book was pretty well known to me. At one stage, I was about thirteen when we went to France with him and he visited some of the aerodromes where he'd been posted during the war. As a schoolboy it seemed rather exciting, though of course what made my family even more of a RAF family is that my uncle Micky was very young when he died.'

Paul Richey didn't talk obsessively or in great detail about the war. 'He certainly wasn't garrulous on the subject but, of course, the book told us a great deal about what he'd done. He was a very brave man and a naturally gifted writer. And his Catholicism was very important to him right until his death.'

There was just one wordless gesture, typical of so many who had flown or worked with Spitfires or other war planes. 'If I was with him, whenever a plane flew overhead, he would just stop. And look up to the sky.'

## Sandals with Wings

The war in Europe was almost over when twenty-three-year-old Harry Ledger stepped inside a Spitfire Mark V for his first ever solo flight. Yet the conflict in the Far East was raging on and Harry would still be flying Spitfires in terrifyingly dangerous missions in the very last hours of the Second World War.

As a toddler, Ledger would send notes up the chimney to Father Christmas. 'Please can I have a pair of winged sandals?' the Oldham schoolboy would write, referring to the stories his father would often read to him about Hermes, the Greek god. His dream of flying, however, seemed increasingly unlikely as he grew up; he'd be joining the family law firm, following in his father's footsteps.

By 1939, when war broke out, Ledger was an eighteen-year-old law student at Manchester University, studying while on deferred service until he got his law degree in 1941. By then, he was firmly determined to fly, despite strong parental opposition: his father wanted to see his son join the firm, and to take up a less hazardous role when he joined the armed services.

Yet when Ledger took his call-up papers to the labour exchange in Rochdale, he was asked if he was interested in aircrew. His response was a resounding yes, despite all his father's misgivings. He signed up to join the RAF without telling his parents he'd be training to fly. 'I think all lads then wanted to fly, really,' Ledger recalled.

His RAF career started in February 1943. 'First I was in London for six weeks, then I was posted to the Initial Training Wing in Cambridge. By June 1943, I got into my first Tiger Moth at grading school near Leicester,' he explained. Then came his first solo flight in a Harvard while stationed in Salisbury, Zimbabwe (then Rhodesia). By this time, he had written to his family and told them he was flying. 'Until then, I'd been so excited about what I was doing. It was only when my roommate got killed in an exercise while we were training there that I realized how dangerous the training could be.' Soon after another young man was killed in training. He had not managed to pull out of a dive. 'But we all just had to get on with it. It was war.'

Harry was at the RAF Operational Training Unit at Fayid, Egypt, for his first ever Spitfire solo training flight on 30 November 1944. 'We'd been flying Harvards until then – a two-seater trainer – and the controls were similar to the Spit. The propeller was adjustable from the cockpit, so there I was, sitting on my parachute, strapped in, and the engine started, ready for take-off. I taxied up to the end of the runway. In a way it was similar to the Harvard. And we set off.'

By that point, Harry had 200 hours' flying time under his belt. 'Flying it didn't seem that different. Raising the undercarriage was a bit of a problem, but it was only when I came into land that it got trickier. There was a notice in the cockpit telling you not to put the undercarriage down if the speed was more than 120 mph, so I shut everything down. But it didn't seem to stop. It was so streamlined, it was as if you were floating along. It was that difficult to get it to slow down. But I wasn't nervous at any point. You'd been taught a method of checking what you should do prior to landing and sure enough, I came down safely.'

A week later, Ledger was told to fly another Mark V up to 20,000 feet and check the oxygen supply. 'But I didn't get round to that. I got up to 10,000 feet and the engine stopped. I didn't panic. I put the nose down a bit, thinking perhaps it would get going again. But it didn't.' Harry called up ground control with a Mayday call, to say the engine had stopped. The call was acknowledged. 'I'd practised forced landings many times, so I pointed the plane towards the aerodrome. I was so at one with the Spit by then, I was pretty sure I could do it. "I'll have to land downwind," I told control. And I was able to land it safely. I didn't really know why the engine had stopped. I was told afterwards it might have been because the engine had backfired through the carburettor and damaged the flame traps. I certainly didn't want to bail out if I could help it.'

After Fayid, Ledger was sent to Karachi, then Bombay, then Poona in western India. At Poona they were equipped with Mark IXs. These new models had a better rate of climb and the engine was more powerful. It also had a four-bladed propeller, instead of the three-blade like the Mark V. But the main thing was that it went up quicker.

In May 1945, Harry joined 155 Squadron, a fighter squadron that served in India and over Burma. Germany had just surrendered and the war in Europe was formally over, but the fight against the Japanese continued. 'In Poona, we went to "Jungle School", learning how to survive if we got shot down. The training finished with a forty-mile trek in extreme heat, a couple of days before we got back to the station.' Harry was also instructed to practise dive-bombing in the Spitfire from 5,000 feet using smoke bombs. 'One of the men training with me was killed during the training, he passed out while doing the dive,' he recalled.

The final days of the war saw Harry engaged in defensive missions in the Burmese jungle. 'By then, in the last months of the Burma campaign, each Spitfire had a 500 lb bomb. We were told to drop our bombs onto the Japanese but I never saw any Japanese, only the trees. But I followed the rest of the squadron and dropped mine where the others had dropped theirs. The bombs had a seven-second delay on them so you could get out of the way. Those were the orders.'

In August 1945, the atom bombs were dropped on Hiroshima and Nagasaki and on 2 September the Japanese surrendered. 'We didn't realize it was all over at the time. We were on a troopship. But by the time the ship reached Singapore, we'd learned it was all over. We had a marvellous time celebrating – it was my birthday, too! There was always that feeling of "How will the war end?" in the background. So when it did, it was a great release.'

Harry continued to fly Dakotas to transport the troops back home until he finally left the RAF in 1946 and returned to Oldham and the family firm. He married his wife, Jean, in 1957. Their daughter, Nancy, went on to follow the family tradition, too, and is still a conveyancing solicitor.

It might have been somewhat brief, but Harry Ledger could be justifiably proud of his time with the Spitfires and 155 Squadron. He was awarded a Burma Star, given to those who were in operational service in the Burma Campaign from 1941 to 1945.

'I've kept my log book and I got a green endorsement – a commendation – for that incident when the Spitfire's engine cut out. The ink's getting a bit faint now.' Those Spitfire memories, however, have been as vivid as if it all happened last week.

## A Black Attaché Case

'In the Polish collection at RAF Northolt, there is a display featuring a small, black, leather attaché case. It is worn. The handle has been repaired with wire. The briefcase was issued to my father, Franciszek Kornicki, as a young cadet at the Polish Air Force Academy in Dęblin, Poland, in 1937,' explained Richard Kornicki, CBE, Chairman of the Polish Air Force Memorial Committee. Franciszek Kornicki flew Spitfires in 315 Squadron and in 317 Squadron. After the Battle of Britain he commanded 317 Squadron, the youngest Polish Air Force commander. 'My father was in the last cohort to complete the three-year course in 1939, just before Hitler's invasion of Poland. By the end of the war, half of those who graduated with him were dead.

'When my father flew in defence of Poland, the black briefcase was under his seat in an open cockpit. When Stalin invaded from the east, my father escaped into Romania to continue the fight from elsewhere, the case his only possession. Avoiding internment in Romania, he escaped by sea to Marseilles, flying in the allied cause until France capitulated. He was evacuated from St Jean de Luz, finally arriving in Liverpool – with the same, small, black briefcase containing nothing much more than just a change of clothes and some papers.

'The case stayed with him throughout his wartime career, which culminated as Officer commanding 317 Squadron and then postwar in the RAF, then in civilian life and finally in retirement as a trustee of the Polish Air Force Association. That simple leather case encapsulates most of my father's adult life. It is also a physical reminder of the odyssey which he and thousands of other Polish airmen made as they fought '*za wolność waszą i naszą*' – for our freedom and yours. At every point on that journey, that attaché case was present.

'It is a witness: it serves to remind people of an extraordinary story, not unique to my father, but experienced by thousands of Poles when war began on 1st September 1939, not 3rd September; whose role in the air war in Britain was critical (the Polish 303 Squadron being the highest-scoring squadron in the Battle of Britain); who were banned by the British government from participating in the 1946 victory parade for fear of offending Stalin; and whose war did not finally end until Communism fell and Poland was once again free, long after peace in the West.

'Those of us who have enjoyed the peace they fought for owe them much. But it is a debt simply paid: by remembering their comrades who never lived to see Germany defeated or Communism collapse. By remembering those who carried injuries for the rest of their lives. By remembering simply that when the RAF flew to defend this country, the Polish Air Force flew with them.'

Franciszek Kornicki was passionate about flying Spitfires: 'You didn't actually fly a Spit, you wore it. It responds so instinctively to your every wish, you only have to think what you want to do and already the aircraft does it for you.'

## The Polish Pilots

The first Polish pilots reached Britain on 8 December 1939, arriving in Eastchurch, Kent, after their departure from France two days earlier. More large transports followed and by early June 1940, 2,164 air personnel had arrived in Britain and been assigned to various squadrons.

France's capitulation on 25 June 1940 forced the Polish Armed Forces, alongside other Allied troops, to withdraw their units to Britain. A further 6,220 Polish air personnel reached Britain by the end of July 1940, increasing the total of Polish airmen on British soil to 8,384. Exhausted Polish servicemen, tired of being defeated by the Germans, looked upon Britain with great anticipation and named it 'The Island of the Last Hope'.

On their part, the British, like the French before them, accepted as truth the German propaganda about Polish

*Above:* Six Spitfire Mark Is of No. 19 Squadron, based at Duxford,
Cambridgeshire, flying in starboard echelon formation.

# YOUR 'SPITFIRES' IN ACTION

*Above:* A boxing contest arranged in aid of a local Supermarine Spitfire fund, 1940.

*Right:* The Leeward Islands are thanked for their donation of funds that helped purchase new Spitfires for Britain.

*Below:* A shopper at London's Lambeth Walk market contributes to the Spitfire fund, 1940.

*Thank you, Leeward Islands!*

*Above: Battle of Britain*, by war artist Paul Nash. Luftwaffe can be seen approaching in formation in the far right-hand corner of the painting.

*Right*: Nash was appointed as a full-time war artist, attached to the RAF and the Air Ministry.

*Left:* Churchill observes a female riveter working on a Spitfire at the Castle Bromwich factory in Birmingham, September 1941.

*Above:* Christine Haig (née Osborne), right, with her father and a friend, in 1934.

*Below:* Eighteen-year-old Christine, after she was called up to work in a Spitfire factory, here with her father (left), who was part of the Home Guard, and her uncle.

# FACTS of the FIGHT for the FACTORY

## SPITFIRE BULLETIN No. 14

TWO FOCKE-WULF 190s DROPPED BOMBS ON A SOUTH COAST TOWN AND HOPED TO GET AWAY UNSCATHED. BUT TWO SPITFIRES WERE AFTER THEM LIKE LIGHTNING. ONLY JUST SKIMMING THE SEA AT OVER 300 M.P.H., THEY CHASED THEM 80 MILES ACROSS THE CHANNEL TO LE HAVRE, SHOT ONE INTO THE SEA AND SMASHED THE OTHER BEYOND HOPE OF ITS LANDING.

THE ENEMY NEVER TURNED TO FIGHT—THEY KNEW BETTER.

SPITFIRES FOR VENGEANCE—AND VICTORY.

—MINISTRY OF AIRCRAFT PRODUCTION.

**THEIR SUCCESS. THEIR CONFIDENCE. THEIR SAFETY** — *They all depend on you*

They need Spares to use their wings

MINISTRY OF AIRCRAFT PRODUCTION.

*Above left:* A Second World War poster supporting aircraft mechanics and repair teams.

*Above right:* Posters like these were put up in aircraft factories around Britain to boost morale.

*Below:* Spitfire fuselages under construction at an aircraft factory in the Midlands.

*Right:* Morale-boosting schemes were introduced to enable workers to see the results of their labours. Here workers from a Spitfire factory examine one of their aircraft at an RAF Fighter Station.

*Left:* Vertical aerial reconnaissance view of the port of Boulogne, taken by a Supermarine Spitfire of the Photographic Reconnaissance Unit.

*Right:* Ninety-one-year-old former strategic photo reconnaissance pilot Jimmy Taylor at Goodwood in 2013, before his flight in the Boultbee Spitfire.

*Above:* Churchill delays his return journey to sit down and talk to Spitfire test pilot Alex Henshaw after an impressive demonstration flight.

*Below*: Flight Sergeant 'Grumpy' Unwin, Flight Lieutenant Lawson and Sergeant Jennings of No. 19 Squadron at Fowlmere, September 1940.

*Left:* WAAF plotters at work in the Operations Room at Headquarters, No. 11 Group, Uxbridge, Middlesex.

*Below*: WAAFs learning how to handle a barrage balloon at the training station at Cardington.

*Below*: Four female ATA pilots (three Americans and one Polish) leaving an airfield near Maidenhead, 19 March 1943.

ineptitude in resisting the German–Soviet invasion and were doubtful about the flying skills of the Polish pilots. Flight Lieutenant John A. Kent, who was posted to No. 303 (Polish) Fighter Squadron during the Battle of Britain, wrote in his memoirs: 'All I knew about the Polish Air Force was that it had lasted about three days against the Luftwaffe, and I had no reason to suppose that they would shine any more brightly operating from England.'

It soon became clear to the British that the Poles were extremely skilled pilots. A total of 145 experienced and battle-hardened Polish airmen fought in the Battle of Britain – 79 airmen in various RAF squadrons, 32 in No. 302 (Polish) Fighter Squadron and 34 in No. 303 (Polish) Fighter Squadron. Polish pilots serving in all RAF squadrons achieved a remarkable score of 203.5 destroyed, 35 probables and 36 damaged. Other sources give 131 kills as there is generally variation in figures for claimed 'kills' – the entire RAF score was lowered from 2,692 to 1,733 aircraft destroyed due to the discrepancy between British and German official figures. Such a feat had a price and twenty-nine Polish pilots lost their lives in combat during the Battle of Britain.

Commander-in-Chief of Fighter Command, Air Chief Marshal Sir Hugh Dowding, once so reluctant to allow Polish pilots into battle, summarized their contribution in the most telling way: 'Had it not been for the magnificent work of the Polish squadrons and their unsurpassed gallantry, I hesitate to say that the outcome of battle would have been the same.'

In June 1941, the Polish pilots started to train on Spitfires.

Throughout the war, the Polish Air Force continued to serve alongside the RAF. Their contribution to the war against Nazi Germany was significant, although achieved at a very heavy price. The 1,903 killed are commemorated at the Polish War Memorial at RAF Northolt where three Polish squadrons had been based during wartime. 'It was an all-Polish station, so quite unique in the Second World War,' recalled Richard Kornicki. 'My father always said Northolt was his second home. The Mess there was so important. It was the only home they had.'

The Polish fighter pilots became well known throughout the war. International journalists flocked to airfields to write about their exploits, waiters refused to take payments for their meals in restaurants, bar owners paid for their drinks and bus conductors allowed them free journeys. Quentin Reynolds, a well-known American war correspondent, dubbed the Polish airmen 'the real Glamor Boys of England' in the magazine *Collier's Weekly*, an apt reflection of the hero-worship attitude the British public had developed towards them.

Such was the celebrity surrounding the Polish fighter pilots, the 315 Squadron airmen were eventually 'adopted' by society hostess and former Hollywood movie star Lady Jersey, the Countess of Richmond. She was the American actress Virginia Cherrill (who had been married briefly to actor Cary Grant) before marrying George Child-Villiers, the 9th Earl of Jersey, in 1937. At the couple's grand country house a few miles from RAF Northolt, Osterley Park and House, Lady Jersey became known as the Polish squadron's 'mother'. 'She would invite them to functions at other grand houses to meet her friends and the Lodge in the grounds of Osterley House was permanently stocked with everything the men would need, so a pilot could have a totally relaxed and comfortable time while on brief leave,' explained Richard Kornicki.

'The Poles did two things that stunned young English girls: they would turn up on a date with flowers – and they would kiss their hand,' said Richard Kornicki. So widely known was the Polish pilots' reputation for gallantry towards the fair sex, there was a much-bandied joke at the time that some British pilots even pretended to be Polish. Apparently their pick-up line was: 'I am a Polish aviator. Please have a drink with me. I am very lonely.'

After the war, some of the Polish airmen settled in Britain and continued their service in the RAF, mostly as flight instructors. Others decided to return to Poland, by then under Soviet occupation. This often had very serious consequences. The Communist regime, distrustful towards ex-servicemen of the Polish Armed Forces in the West, barred them from flying in the Polish Air Force and in numerous cases, imprisoned them on trumped up espionage charges. One of the most drastic cases was of Wing Commander Stanisław Skalski, the top Polish scorer of the war, who spent eight years in prison after initially being sentenced to death. It was not until Stalin's death in 1953 that most of the airmen were able to regain their ranks and serve again in the Polish Air Force.

## The Lucky Kiwi

Alan Deere was born in Auckland, New Zealand, in December 1917. He was working as a law clerk in Whanganui when he joined the RAF in 1937 and after training was posted to 54 Squadron at RAF Hornchurch. In May 1940, when his squadron was assigned to cover the evacuation of the British Expeditionary Force from Dunkirk, Deere destroyed six Luftwaffe planes in the course of just one week and was shot down himself – returning to base nineteen hours later after hitching a ride on a boat across the Channel. For this he was awarded the DFC (Distinguished Flying Cross) presented to him by King George VI in June 1940. Yet this was only the beginning of Deere's extraordinary record.

During the Battle of Britain, Deere's squadron was part of No. 11 Group, the first RAF Fighter Command group to be formed, responsible for the air defence of Southern England, including London. Commanded by another New Zealander, Air Vice Marshall Keith Park, No. 11 Group bore the brunt of the German aerial assault against London and the southeast. Between July and September 1940, Deere shot down another eight planes, earning him another DFC (Bar) in the process. Yet he came very close to losing his life in that period.

In July 1940, Deere's squadron was scrambled to intercept an enemy formation near Dover. They discovered a group of Messerschmitt Bf 109 fighters escorting a seaplane, sent to undertake pre-invasion surveys of the English coast. Deere's section immediately engaged the fighter escort and the New Zealander quickly sent a Bf 109 down in flames. He was manoeuvring to attack another fighter when a German plane suddenly headed straight for him. Locked in a deadly game of 'chicken' neither pilot gave way and the aircraft collided, badly damaging Deere's engine. Unable to bail out and with his cockpit filling with smoke, he managed to head inland and crash land.

His Spitfire came to rest in the middle of a cornfield, and he managed to smash his way out before the plane burst into flames. He walked away with minor cuts and burns and was back on patrol the very next day.

A few weeks later, Alan Deere was shot down again. He'd pursued a Bf 109 across the Channel and shot it down near Calais, only to be attacked by five German fighters. Outnumbered, he was able to evade his pursuers long enough to reach the English coast, but was forced to bail out of his bullet-ridden Spitfire. 'Bullets seemed to come from everywhere and pieces flew off my aircraft. Never did it take so long to cross the Channel. Then my Spitfire burst into flames, so I undid my straps and eased the stick back to gain height before bailing out. Turned my machine on its back and pushed the stick hard forward. I shot out a few feet but somehow became caught up. Although I twisted and turned, I could not free myself. The nose of my aircraft had now dropped and was pointing at the ground, which was rushing up at an alarming rate. Then suddenly I was blown along the side of the fuselage and was clear. A hurried snatch at the rip cord and, with a jolt, the parachute opened.'

As the Luftwaffe raids over England intensified in late August 1940, Deere and fellow New Zealanders Colin

Gray (later Group Captain) and Johnny Gibson (later Squadron Leader) quickly established themselves as a trio of outstanding fighter pilots. Moreover, Deere's run of good luck continued to hold.

On 28 August 1940, he was forced to bail out over the Kent countryside, landing in the middle of a fully laden plum tree – much to the annoyance of a local farmer.

Three days later, 54 Squadron's airfield at Hornchurch was bombed, just as Deere was preparing to take off. Shrapnel tore off a wing and the propeller of his Spitfire, flipping the aircraft over and sending it sliding along the airfield upside down. Deere was dragged out by another pilot who promptly collapsed and had to be carried to safety – by none other than Deere!

Rested in December 1940, Deere had a spell as an operations room controller before returning to operational duty in May 1941 with 602 Squadron. Based in Scotland, he was one of the pilots scrambled on 10 May to investigate reports of a lone German plane flying towards Glasgow. He did not make contact with the aircraft, which later made a forced landing on the outskirts of the city. Later, it was revealed that the pilot was deputy Nazi Party leader Rudolf Hess. (Hess, whose real motives for flying to Scotland in the middle of the war remain somewhat baffling, was imprisoned and eventually sent for trial at Nuremburg in 1946, where he was found guilty for crimes against peace, and conspiracy with other German leaders to commit crimes. He took his own life in August 1987, aged ninety-three, in Spandau Prison.)

In January 1942, Deere embarked on a short tour of

the USA to teach fighter tactics to American pilots. Three months later, he took command of a Canadian Spitfire squadron before being posted to RAF Biggin Hill in February 1943 as Wing Leader. Over the next six months he led 121 sorties and earned the DSO (Distinguished Service Order). He went on to command the Free French fighter wing through D-Day and the liberation of France before returning to staff duty in England. He finished the war as New Zealand's second highest-scoring air ace – behind Colin Gray – with 22 confirmed victories, 10 probable and 18 damaged.

## THE BATTLE OF BRITAIN

In 1940, Hitler sent 2,600 Luftwaffe fighters and bombers to destroy the Royal Air Force. At the start of the battle, the RAF had 640 fighter planes – Hurricanes and Spitfires – and Luftwaffe Commander in Chief Hermann Göring confidently predicted victory within a few days. Britain stepped up production of fighter planes. The Hurricanes, with sturdy frames, took on the German bombers. The Mark I Spitfires, with superior speed and agility, were sent up to shoot down German fighters. At the start of the battle, nineteen squadrons of RAF Fighter Command were equipped with Spitfires. By the end of the battle, the better organized and lead RAF had defeated the Luftwaffe and downed 1,887 German planes. The RAF had lost 1,023 fighter planes, 376 bombers, with 148 from Coastal Command also lost – a total of 1,547.

In May 1945, Deere was awarded an OBE and continued to have a prestigious postwar career, including service as aide-de-camp to Queen Elizabeth II in 1962. The Lucky Kiwi had become The Queen's Man. He died in September 1995, aged seventy-seven. Fittingly, his ashes were scattered over the River Thames. From a Spitfire, of course.

## Tip 'em Up Terry

Terry Spencer was born in Bedford in 1918. After an engineering degree at the University of Birmingham, he joined the Royal Engineers in 1939, only to transfer to the RAF in 1941. After training, he was posted to his first operational unit, 26 Squadron at Gatwick in November 1942. In June 1943, he was promoted to Flight Commander of the unit and four months later to Flight Lieutenant (WS). He started flying Spitfires at the end of that year. 'In December 1943, I achieved my ambition to get on to Spitfires, the most beautiful aircraft in the world and the most wonderful to fly. On my very first operation as a Number Two to the Commanding Officer at 165 Squadron, I crash-landed at Ford as my undercart failed to lock down. Little damage to the Spit and none to me, but not a propitious start.

'We did long hours on "cockpit readiness", which involved being strapped in, prepared to scramble at a second's notice. On one such occasion my windscreen oiled up and I had to take off with the hood open only to have an engine cut at 10,000 feet, fortunately right above the aerodrome.

'One-six-five Spit Squadron flew many sorties after German aircraft but they were few and far between so we concentrated on low-level strafing [repeated attacks with bombs or machine gun fire from low-flying aircraft] and shipping patrols in the Bay of Biscay and the English Channel. The evenings saw hectic parties and one evening I walked through a plate glass door in the Mess and was given three stitches by the squadron doctor, who had had as much to drink as all of us. That party ended at a quarter to six in the morning.'

In May 1944, Terry was posted as 'A' Flight Commander to 41 Squadron. 'At the beginning, it was difficult for me as most of the other pilots had considerably more operational experience. The clipped-wing Spit XIIs were much faster than the older IXBs and much nicer to handle.

'At RAF Bolt Head (near Salcombe, Devon) I met a most attractive girl from the operations room. I could share my problems with her as we strolled along the cliffs on beautiful moonlit nights. Our radios when flying were transmitted through loudspeakers all over the ops room and the language those girls heard when things got tough was enough to make any of them blush. I used to meet my girl most nights when she came off duty.

'A dawn flight saw me leading six aircraft to St Malo, flying across the channel just a few feet off the water. We hit Sillon de Talbert and eventually finished up at Ushant. A very poor show, which depressed me considerably, especially as I had been sent to 41 Squadron as an expert in low-level navigation. To make matters worse, a great pal of mine, David Bell, was shot down off St Malo. He was on fire and failed to bail out.

'A dilemma occurred when my Number Two was shot down off St Peter Port in the Channel Islands. Wag was one of the few Americans in the RAF. Most had transferred to the American Air Force as their pay was almost double ours. Wag bailed out and got into his dinghy. A Warwick aircraft dropped him a Lindholme rescue craft (also known as a Lindholme dinghy, comprising a string of five containers, one with an eight-man rubber dinghy, the others with various items like food, signals and clothing) and I saw a German patrol boat go out to pick him up. I could have shot up the boat but felt if I did he would be left to drown. The Huns picked him up but my Spit was hit several times by heavy flak and I had to leave him to become a prisoner of war. Thirty years later, I was invited to a party in London where I met Wag, whom I had last seen in the drink off St Peter Port. He said he had never forgiven me for leaving him to be taken prisoner. However, years later, my wife Lesley and I stayed with Wag and his wife Brooke in Baltimore and remained good friends ever since.

'In June 1944, I had just said goodnight to my ops room girl and tumbled into bed and was fast asleep when the CO woke me up to say the invasion of Europe was on. The rest of the night was spent in the ops room organizing patrols and I myself took off at dawn to witness the most spectacular sight of my life: the Channel was littered with thousands of boats – from warships to landing craft – all heading towards the French coast at Normandy. Our job was to combat enemy aircraft, but we saw none that day. Returning from a later sortie my main petrol cock jammed and I was about to bail out at 500 feet off the sea when a feverish kick partially released it and produced enough petrol to get me back to Bolt Head at 85 mph – just off the stall.

'Later that month we received news that we were to go to West Malling to cope with the latest German secret weapon, the flying bomb, so very sadly I said goodbye to my ops room girl. The doodlebugs, as the flying bombs were nicknamed, flew at 420 mph and at 4,000 feet. Shooting at these high speeds required new techniques. The Spit had to be very accurately trimmed to avoid any skidding in the turns or our fire power was inaccurate. We learned not to attack from dead astern: when I once did, the flying bomb exploded 250 yards ahead of me and blew my Spit upside down, causing immense damage as I crashed through the debris. We were fascinated with these doodlebugs and one such missile, flying relentlessly up the Thames, received all the ammunition of Flight Sergeant Chattin and myself. We slowed it down to 220 mph, enabling me to fly alongside and take a close look. With my wingtip two feet from the bomb, it began to lift. This toppled its gyro and it crashed harmlessly into the water below. I became a bit of a hero that night in the British press as "Tip 'em up Terry", the first man to topple a flying bomb with my wingtip, although I never actually touched the bomb and really it was due to lousy shooting.

'One of these doodlebugs dropped onto the RAF Regiment's billets. I helped drag out the CO with his brains blown out. After this, eight of us climbed aboard my two-seater Le Mans Singer, known as "the Blue Peril", and headed for London to party and forget about the realities of war. The Singer was beautifully maintained by my engine

TIP 'EM UP TERRY IN 1944. — — TOM SLACK 87.

fitter who used it himself and ensured it was always full of 100 octane petrol. It was never taxed or insured throughout the war. Its canvas hood had long since rotted and we were all open to the elements.

'Paris was recaptured on 23 August 1944 and soon afterwards we saw the ill-fated airborne invasion of Arnhem when we escorted the massive armada of gliders and paratroopers. Our job was to attack German gun positions as they opened fire on the fleet. This was not dangerous as we attacked them from the rear; but we did not envy our poor Red Devils (the Parachute Regiment) having to drop or land in that holocaust while we headed home to our girlfriends and comfortable beds. About this time I took a Spit to see my ops room girl but was told she had just gone to Plymouth – 500 miles to be told that!

'When based at RAF Lympne, Kent, we had many fine parties at Ann Attree's house. Ann had run the Lympne Flying Club before 1939. She was a wonderful character, much loved by all the pilots. One night we crammed her into the Blue Peril with four other pilots to go drinking in Folkestone. At a bar someone put a condom in her long "bread roll" (a popular upswept hairdo of the time). Ann kept tugging at the roll until admitting defeat. She opened the roll and discovered what we had done. She never forgave us.

'From Lympne I took a Spit IX 5R-Z up on an air test and was not happy with the engine when it cut out on me at 400 feet as I was coming in to land with wheels and flaps fully down. I crashed into a wood running up the side of a hill when the wings were torn off and the engine broke away from the airframe. The fire crew were somewhat surprised to pass me walking up the road back to the 'drome quite unscathed.

'The Battle of Arnhem was followed by large formations of fighters escorting American Flying Fortresses bombing heavily defended Ruhr industrial areas in Germany. Our Spits were usually top cover and we looked down on the dreadful turmoil below as the bombers flew through dense clouds of aircraft fire. Some blew up and disgorged their human contents, with a few fortunates gliding earthwards on billowing white parachutes while others, as tiny dots in the sky, hurtled to their deaths.

'At this period of the war we were leading lives outside reality. On the one hand, we were engaged in deadly aerial combat and, on the other, returning to a world that had seen little of the actual fighting other than the bombing – all in a matter of hours. This tended to set us apart from our fellow humans when neither could understand the other.

'On a raid in the Liege area, we attacked two Focke-Wulf

190s at Tirlemont in Belgium. I shot one down in flames and he blew up on hitting the ground. I was promptly bounced by the other who shattered my starboard elevator and wing. W/O [Warrant Officer] Coleman got him but only after W/O Chattin was himself shot down. He bailed out. I saw his Spit hit the deck.

'Fifty years later, John Foreman, an aviation historian, told me the man I shot down was Hauptmann Emil Lang. Lang was the top-scoring fighter ace of the Luftwaffe, having claimed 173 Allied aircraft destroyed. His wingman, Lieutenant Alfred Gross, shot down W/O Chattin then, in turn, was shot down by W/O Coleman. Gross was also a top-scoring air ace, having shot down 29 Allied aircraft, but he was so badly wounded he never returned to combat and died three years later. Foreman sent me a photo of Lang who looked a hell of a nice guy.

'It took me fifty years fully to understand this tragedy and the anguish of his mother, wife or girlfriend. Up to that time the war had been totally impersonal to me.

'John Foreman also told me that Chattin was killed, possibly by Germans, after he landed by parachute. On landing back from that trip we watched helplessly as one of our sergeant pilots was burnt to death after he overturned on landing. Only a drink could eradicate that memory. Then we laughed and washed the event out of our minds.

'The next morning I nicked the Station Commander's Tiger Moth for the weekend to visit my father in the Isle of Wight. On the Monday morning Dad drove me back to the field where a strong gale was blowing. I co-opted three villagers to hold the tail and wing down as I swung the prop.

When I waved my arm, they were all to let go, but the two on the wing held on. A sudden gust under the tail overturned the plane making it a total write-off! A short time after this event, a wild party took place in the Sergeants' Mess. In the early hours of the morning we strung a rope around the dancers on the floor and with a tug on the rope, heaved on it, squeezing in the dancers until they couldn't move, to the laughter of those of us outside the rope. W/O Jimmy Ware hit a corporal and when another W/O came up to complain to me bitterly, I hit him – in my drunken state. We stole a 15 hundredweight truck and drove back to the Officers' Mess to continue the party until dawn. What a night!

'The next morning there was a great stink about the party. A few weeks later I had to fly up to Biggin Hill to get a reprimand from 11 Group AOC [Air Officer Commanding]. This was for the Tiger Moth incident. Air Commodore Bouchier was in 41 Squadron before 1939 and for an hour we talked about the squadron. After I had reached the headquarter gates on my way out, his ADC [aide-de-camp] ran out to announce the AOC had forgotten to give me the reprimand. I returned rather sheepishly to see a smiling AOC. But those were the last few days of Bouchier. When I went back again a few days later to get a reprimand for the dance floor incident, I was met by a very different AOC. After he had finished haranguing me for "behaviour unbecoming to an officer", he ended by saying he would never allow me to command a squadron.

'During the bitter winter of 1944/5 as we tried to keep up with the Allied advance across Europe, I left my beloved 41 to command 350 Belgian Squadron flying the latest Spit

XIVs, but not before reminding Group Captain "Johnnie" Johnson what the AOC had told me. Johnnie was the top-scoring Allied fighter pilot of the Second World War and highly decorated. "Fuck the AOC," said Johnnie. "We have a war on our hands."'

Low-level strafing in Germany was becoming a dicey business. 'This was reflected in our casualties,' Terry recalled. 'We had to strafe locomotives and transport in the heavily defended Ruhr. This involved flying through the balloon barrage and "flak" that at times was so intense it seemed impossible that any aircraft could survive it. Our Spitfires often resembled colanders after these trips. We soon developed a technique but it was a tricky one. The Spit XIV had a tremendous rate of climb and we would climb at 8,000 feet a minute at only 90 mph. The German gunners could not calibrate their guns down to this low speed but it meant we were continually flying into the flak without getting hit.

'Once based on the Continent, we were encouraged to visit our Army colleagues in the front-line trenches. These men lived for days on end in frozen water and unbelievable cold: they were constantly shelled and seemed to take it all as routine. We watched the Germans shelling a nearby village when a shell fell within 30 yards of us. The four visiting pilots threw themselves flat on their faces to the laughter of the Army boys.

'The weather conditions for our last Christmas in Belgium were atrocious. We regularly had to climb up through some 10,000 feet of cloud when we formatted with wing tips a mere three feet apart. The slipstream helped keep us in tight formation. On Christmas Day, leading the dawn patrol, we chased the Germans' latest jet fighter, the Me 262 (Messerschmitt fighter-bomber), but though we dived on him at 500 mph we could not catch him.

'On New Year's Day the Germans reckoned the British would have huge hangovers and launched their biggest aerial attack ever on our grounded fighters. We had taken off at first light and seen nothing until returning to find many of our Spits in flames on the air strip. Once in Germany, we shot up everything that moved. Unlike in France, Belgium and Holland, where we had to be careful of civilians and even do dummy runs before attacking trains to let the civilians escape, at the same time alerting the German gunners, now we had a free hand. As the war was ending, we had plenty of Spitfires but pilots were scarce as no one wanted to get killed so close to the end of it all. Some tried to avoid taking off by blowing radio fuses, until we told them they would have to take off without radio. That put an end to it.'

All this came to an abrupt end for Terry on 26 February 1945 when he was shot down attacking ground targets near Münster in Germany. 'I had time to climb to 8,000 feet, by which time the cockpit was full of smoke and uncomfortably hot. I called Roberto Muls, my Number Two, that I was on fire and bailing out. Unfortunately, I then hit the tailplane and injured my hip. I felt no pain, only a serene calm as I drifted gently down to earth beneath the silken canopy. The peace and quiet after the turmoil seemed like another world until I remembered I was falling into the hands of Germans who had little love for Allied fighter pilots.

'I landed in a field beside some French slave workers but was promptly surrounded by gun-toting German soldiers shouting and gesticulating at me. They took me to a military hospital where my hip was treated and then deposited me in a freezing prison cell. I spent the next two weeks in solitary confinement – lonely, cold, hungry and miserable before being taken to the air crew interrogation centre at Oberusal, outside Frankfurt. During the early hours of the morning on Frankfurt station, I lost my guards. It was dark and miserably cold. I approached several German civilians announcing "*Ich bin Kriegsgefanger*" [I am a prisoner of war] but they thought I was joking. Eventually, at the camp an arrogant major scowled. "You arrived in our country uninvited and dressed in civilian clothes (we often flew in sweaters and I was not wearing a tunic). If you will not talk to me, I will hand you over to the Gestapo who will make you talk." I felt very alone when realizing that no one knew I was alive. The major stressed that point.'

But the war was coming to an end. 'The next night there was a heavy Allied bombing raid on Wetzlar and German civilians streamed into our POW camp thinking they would be safe. In the mêlée Jimmy Thiele, a New Zealander, and I slipped through the main gate just for the hell of it. Once outside the barbed wire, Jimmy turned round to me and said, "Fuck going back inside". We had not planned to escape and had no equipment beyond my silk scarf, which was a map of Europe, and Jimmy's tunic button, containing a mini compass. We walked west all night and at dawn met a French slave worker who gave us a 98cc motorcycle saying it was no use to him as he could not get petrol. But there was a Hungarian unit down the road with plenty of petrol. The Hungarians wore khaki and so did we. We stole a couple of trays and queued up for food, the first proper food we had had in weeks – and were promptly sick!

'There were so many foreigners trudging eastwards that no one took heed of us. More vital was a stack of jerrycans [petrol containers]. We removed one which would take us to the Rhine. Later that afternoon, as we headed west, we heard firing just ahead and dived for a culvert with our precious motorbike. An armoured vehicle rattled overhead, firing wildly. We rode on, balanced precariously on our jerrycan, passing several dead bodies beside the road. On entering an apparently deserted village, we were pounced on by heavily armed Americans. Without identification we were arrested but managed to slip out of the back of the house, collect our motorbike and head for the Rhine once more.

'General Patton had just crossed the Rhine at Remagen – and so did we! We hitched back to our wing, now in Holland, and entered Johnnie Johnson's caravan, where he exclaimed, "Terry! Where the bloody hell have you been these last five weeks?"'

Incredibly, Terry's last months of the war saw him being captured a second time. On 19 April, he was leading a section of four Belgian Spitfires attacking a tanker in the Bay of Wismar in the Baltic in the late evening. His Spitfire was shot down by a German destroyer and he wound up in the sea, his parachute canopy collapsed above him as he struggled to swim beneath it. He was a prisoner of war for the second time, but events were on his side: his camp was liberated after a couple of weeks and he rejoined his Wing soon after.

By this time, he had already started to consider his future. What held most appeal was the itinerant life of a freelance photographer. The war itself had already given him a powerful desire for adventure and, as he realized later, his RAF experience provided excellent training for such a life. 'It gave me quick reactions, taught me survival and the discipline to go one way towards trouble when the temptation was to do the opposite. Over the years to come, I was prepared to take risks to get pictures but only if there was a strong chance of success.'

Terry's demob came through at Christmas 1945. He'd been awarded a DFC and a Belgian Croix de Guerre avec Palme. In February 1946, he agreed to deliver a Proctor, a small single-engined aeroplane, to South Africa. 'It had no radio, no dinghy or emergency supplies for the 8,000-mile flight and there were maps only as far as Cairo. But it was a job,' Terry said.

After refuelling in Marseilles and the hairiest of flights, Terry and the Proctor arrived in Johannesburg, South Africa. The job, however, did not end there. For several months, he continued to fly in Africa as a personal pilot to a successful diamond merchant. Then fate stepped in. A friend in London suggested Terry look up a 'Lesley Brook' who had recently arrived in Johannesburg from England.

'Women were in short supply in Jo'burg at the time,' said Terry of that first meeting in a hotel lobby. 'I waited anxiously at the lift. Imagine my surprise when quite the loveliest girl I have ever seen stepped out. She wore a silk floral dress and displayed an elegant pair of legs. She was wearing a simple gold necklace, had grey-blue eyes and was about five foot five inches tall. Her hair was fair and French-rolled at the back.'

Lesley Brook had left behind a successful career as a stage and film actress in England to make a new life for herself in South Africa. She had understudied Vivien Leigh and played the lead role in over twenty films, working with many well-known actors. During the war she went on tour with ENSA (Entertainments National Service Association), the wartime organization set up to provide entertainment for the armed forces. Yet like so many others, she opted to leave England's grey postwar gloom to make an adventurous journey into the unknown southern hemisphere.

Two days after arriving in Johannesburg, she stepped out of the hotel lift to meet Terry. Just a few weeks later, Terry proposed. 'To my amazement she said "Yes",' recalled Terry. 'We drank champagne, toasting ourselves to a long life together.'

And so it was – for sixty-two years. The pair returned briefly to England to marry and went back to South Africa where they bought a small farm, raised a family and Terry launched an aerial photography business. Throughout the fifties, Terry became much in demand as a photojournalist for *Life* magazine, covering Africa's hot spots and later Vietnam, the Middle East and photographing many other major events and political crises around the world. Often he was away for months at a time, leaving Lesley to raise their daughters Cara (born in 1949) and Raina (born 1958) single-handedly, in what were quite primitive conditions. Tragedy struck the family hard when their four-year-old son, Sean, drowned in an unfenced children's swimming pool in 1956.

In 1962, after fifteen years in Africa, the Spencers returned to live in England. As the beginnings of Beatlemania took hold, Terry spent several months photographing the group for *Life* magazine, riding with them in their cars, eating with them in small tucked away cafes, following them into recording studios. When *Life* magazine folded in 1972, Terry continued to freelance for a range of publications including the *New York Times*.

Lesley and Terry spent their last decade living in Hampshire. They continued to travel frequently and enjoy life to the full. In February 2009, they died within twenty-four hours of each other – Lesley just days away from her ninety-first birthday, Terry nearly ninety. 'I probably saw as much action working for *Life* as I did in three years flying for the RAF in the Second World War,' Terry reflected in 2002. 'One thing was sure, if I'd had to lead my life over again, I would not have changed it.'

## Parachute Poker

Edward Ernest Vine, known as 'Bill', was born in Liverpool in 1921. He'd carried out his basic flying training in Alabama, in the USA, under what was known as the Arnold Scheme, established to train British RAF pilots in the USA. He had only recently arrived in Malta with 1435 Squadron in January 1943.

On 3 March, on take-off, he and three other Spitfires

from the squadron, led by their CO, Squadron Leader W. A. Smith, formed in line abreast formation and climbed steadily to about 25,000 feet, approaching the coast. At this point, their Malta controller warned them there were bandits (enemy aircraft) climbing towards them. In fact, the Bf 109s were 4,000 feet above them. The six Bf 109s caught the four Spitfires in a classic bounce, high in the Sicilian sky about 6 miles south of the enemy airfield at Comiso, Sicily. One of the other pilots, Pilot Officer McDougall, was immediately shot down. His wing man, Pilot Officer Taggart, took hits as well. He managed to turn back towards Malta and ditched in the narrow channel between the two islands.

Bill Vine got ready to deal with one of the enemy machines and gave chase, but was quickly intercepted by one of the other 109s which managed to hit his Spit in the engine. Like many Spit variants it had two fuel tanks, an upper which contained 48 gallons of aviation fuel and a lower with 37 gallons, both located directly in front of the pilot immediately behind the instrument panel.

'I lost power and almost immediately my aircraft caught fire – a rather dodgy situation. The fire spread rapidly into the cockpit and my only chance was to bail out.' Vine's predicament was, to say the least, unenviable. In such circumstances, pilots were advised to slide the cockpit canopy fully open, disconnect oxygen and R/T [radio transmit] leads, then undo the harness. With nothing to keep them in the cockpit, they should roll the Spitfire onto its back and push the stick forward, with the resulting G-force popping them out like a cork out of a bottle. As with many such procedures – easier said than done!

It took Bill Vine three attempts before he finally managed to get clear. 'I am sure that rolling over and pushing the stick forward worked admirably in normal circumstances. On the other hand, with the cockpit on fire and getting warmer by the second, shielding the face from the flames with one hand and endeavouring to disengage the leads and cockpit harness – and alert to the fact that the best part of a tank of high octane fuel was ready to explode – made it rather tiresome!

'To be honest, to this day, I don't remember how I got out. I do recall after one attempt thinking that I wasn't going to make it. I almost relaxed and accepted things until something forced me up to try once again. I really think that the Spitfire exploded and discharged me, as the next thing I remember was spinning around in the air, minus flying helmet, boots and with my tunic and trousers on fire.' As he fell and before the parachute opened, Bill remembered that some of his friends back in Malta used to say that he would be lucky if his parachute ever opened because he was always poking at its corners. And, of course, it might very well have been damaged in the attack or by the cockpit fire. But, to his relief, it opened as it should. To the burnt and wounded Vine 'the crack of the 'chute opening was very welcome.'

But then, just as it seemed he might survive, one of the 109s came back and circled him. Obviously, Vine wondered if the German pilot might shoot him, or try to collapse the canopy – such things did happen – but Vine landed safely in the inshore shallows, to be picked up shortly afterwards by some Italian soldiers. 'I was in a rather sorry state, with a badly burnt face, splinters in my foot and was eventually carted off to hospital. The German who had circled me did come to see me in hospital – and we shook hands!'

The Germans and Italians debated who should keep the downed pilot. The Germans won the argument and Vine spent the rest of the war as a prisoner. Bill returned to the UK safely in 1945, but only after having endured one of the terrible winter marches of Allied prisoners from Poland to eastern Germany and Heydekrug, East Prussia (now Lithuania), from where he was liberated. The prison camps, holding thousands of Allied troops, had been emptied and the inhabitants were forced to march in terrible conditions, led by Germans forces, many of whom would have known that defeat was imminent. Thousands perished in such marches, through hunger, cold and brutality.

Bill Vine died in Cumbria, on 7 July 2006, aged eighty-five.

## A TRUE GENT

For the rest of his life, Bill's face bore the scars of his disastrous last flight, the line of his oxygen mask discernable. Normally, he had flown with the cockpit canopy cracked open – it wasn't unknown for them to jam on the rails – but he didn't wear goggles, believing that they restricted his vision. Had he worn them, his facial burns might have been less severe.

He was, said his friend Bill Simpson in tribute, a kindly man with a pawky (sardonic) sense of humour. He was philosophical about what had happened to him during the war – a gentleman in every sense of the word.

# CHAPTER 4

# On the Ground

IT WAS HARD WORK AND LONG days, but the ground crew of the RAF kept the Spitfires in the air throughout the war. From cleaning and servicing the aircraft, to repairs and refuelling, to dealing with constant air raids and extremely basic living quarters, the aircraft men and women worked tirelessly to keep their kites in top condition and ready for battle. In these compelling stories, we get a sense of their commitment and focus, but also the pride of those that worked with the Spitfire pilots to ensure victory for the Allied forces.

## How to Clean a Spitfire

Edward ('Ted') Sadler was twenty when he responded to a newspaper advertisement to join the RAF in January 1941. After training, he became a Group 1 tradesman (Fitter IIA, Rank AC1) and was delighted to receive his very first posting as a Flight Mechanic to RAF Benson, Oxfordshire – just 9 miles from his home. 'I didn't think I could have enjoyed a service job more than I did that of Fitter IIA. The training I'd received taught me many things and gave me more confidence in my ability working on Spits. I enjoyed being out in the sun, working on "my" kite, proud to keep it serviced and clean, as I had to sign the maintenance schedule each day to certify its airworthiness. Having the power to decide whether in my opinion it was fit to fly was a responsibility I didn't take lightly.

'I used to lean on the tailplane with my arm resting on the fuselage just in front of the fin and look along the graceful lines of 'my' Spit. My keenness had an unfortunate outcome the day I cleaned it with a mixture of oil and petrol, which gave it a brilliant shine. As it took off for a photographic mission over France, I followed its progress with pride, as far as I could see. Then I returned to the maintenance hangar to await its return. Eagerly, I approached the Spit as it landed, stepped up onto the wing to help the pilot. "Who cleaned this kite?" he asked as he slid back the hood. "I did, sir," I said proudly. "Well, don't bloody do it again. It shines like a sixpence up a sweep's backside. I've been chased by every Hun over France!"

'My ego suddenly and thoroughly deflated. I could understand his concern as he flew over enemy territory alone, shining in the sun with no means of defending himself. I never did it again. Fortunately, we were later issued with a cleaning fluid that left a matt finish, so I was still able to take pride in my kite.'

## Ken's Last Wish

Ken Farlow had barely turned nineteen when he found himself crammed with thousands of other men in the

SPITFIRE STORIES

sweltering belly of a troop ship in a convoy, dodging U-boats for seven weeks. He'd joined the RAF in May 1940, an eighteen-year-old from Wath-upon-Dearne, a small town in the West Riding of Yorkshire.

Leaving school at fourteen, Ken started out helping install electric lighting into council houses and soon qualified as an electrician. Nine months after war was declared he signed up with the RAF, where he remained for six years as an electrical engineer working on Hurricanes, Spitfires, Wellington bombers and Kittyhawks.

Initially with 38 Squadron in the Middle East, he spent three years in the North African desert and in Syria with the RAF's 450 Squadron, supporting the front-line forces before returning to England with 91 Squadron towards the end of the war.

'He was constantly on the move. In one month alone, they changed bases six times! They lived in tents or trenches in the baking heat of day and the freezing cold of night, without fresh drinking water because of the dead bodies – animal and human – the enemy had dumped in wells. Mugs of tea often came with a generous layer of grit at the bottom,' said Ken's son, author and academic Andrew Farlow. 'Using captured or hastily constructed airfields, they were very vulnerable. He told us a story how three sudden, screeching black dots, skimming the horizon, headed straight towards him, in open desert, with nowhere to hide. They were Messerschmitts. He could almost touch their wings. They blew apart two of his mates and the plane they were all working on. He'd been working in the cockpit of the plane just a few minutes before – he could have easily died with them.'

124

'Ken told us the story of a friend killed by a booby-trap mine that was set off by vibrations as they worked,' Andrew recalled. 'He also told us of the night he trembled with fear at the bottom of a trench as a bomb was dropped and he was showered with dirt as it thudded into the ground just feet away.' Ken didn't always escape without injury himself. 'He'd helped to rescue crew from crippled planes, or pull their mangled bodies out if they didn't make it,' Andrew revealed. 'He spent several weeks blindfolded, fearing the loss of his eyesight after an exploding battery sprayed acid deep into his eyes. And he also got severe malaria, hallucinated badly and nearly died.'

While waiting to be demobbed, Ken had volunteered for the Mountain Rescue Service. 'One of his jobs was to help retrieve bodies from aircraft that had crashed in the Scottish Highlands, putting them onto the backs of donkeys whose noses were tied with rags dipped in strong spirits to mask the smell. But he also told us one of the most precious moments of his life was arriving home when he was demobbed. Standing in the hallway, he could hear his family upstairs, laughing and chatting excitedly, getting ready for his arrival. He breathed in the beauty of the moment, called out, and they came tearing down the stairs in tears of joy to envelop him in their arms.'

After the war, Ken worked as a chartered electrical engineer on nuclear power stations and also for what was known as the Central Electricity Generating Board (until the national supply of electricity was privatized in the 1990s). He married Jean in 1962 and they and their three children, Andrew, Helen and Adrian, eventually settled in Gloucestershire in 1974.

Over the years, Ken remained silent about his wartime experiences. In fact, his children only learned of them when he was in his late eighties. 'It was only after our mum died in 2007 that he started talking about it. Mum always said to him, "Oh, stop banging on about the war." So he did,' explained his daughter Helen. 'He didn't feel he was a hero, with friends and families being killed through the Blitz. He said it didn't feel right to get any medals or anything like that. He'd say: "All those people that died, they didn't get any medals." He was very much a Yorkshire man – proud and stubborn.'

Ken was ninety-three when the Farlow family learned he had colon cancer. 'We moved him to sheltered accommodation in Painswick. By 2016, he was bedridden for a while and we thought we might lose him. So I asked him, in a roundabout way, what would he like to see. He mentioned a few things and then he said he'd love to see the Spitfire again.'

Helen and her husband got to work. This was her father's last wish and she was determined to fulfil it. She spotted a local event on Facebook: the Spitfire would be making an appearance at Gloucestershire Airport in June for Armed Forces Day.

'We decided to take him for a surprise trip. Before the flight time we took him to the Aviator pub for a drink and he met some pilots from the Battle of Britain Memorial Flight. They spent a long time chatting to Dad, listening to his stories about North Africa and other places. Then we took him to watch the Spitfires through the wired fence as their engines started up and they taxied down the runway for the flyover. It was a wonderful couple of hours for Dad.'

Back at home, Helen sent the poignant photo of Ken watching the Spitfires through the fence, with his story, to a local newspaper, and the story took flight. The director of Gloucestershire Airport then contacted Helen to say he'd organized a VIP tour at RAF Coningsby for Ken, another hugely enjoyable experience for him, followed by a second VIP trip to the Royal International Air Tattoo at Fairford. 'He spent the whole day at the Tattoo, watching every display and being pushed around in his wheelchair, chatting all the time to ground crew and flight engineers. It all turned into an amazing, exciting rollercoaster of a ride for Dad and us – all from just one photo. When he talked to the pilots and the engineers he'd say it was the engine itself, the components, that made the plane such a success. It was so wonderful for Dad to be talking to the same people who are now doing the job he did in the 1940s.'

Ken died in November 2016 with his family around him. 'We were so lucky to be able to give him those experiences. Dad was never ever self-pitying. As he got frailer, instead of cussing he just got on with it. He would often say to us: "I'm one of the lucky ones".'

## Kittie's Long Weight

The Supermarine Seafire, the Naval version of the Spitfire, was adapted for operation from aircraft carriers. It was first used in combat during the Allied landings in North Africa in November 1942. The Seafire provided cover during the Allied invasion of Sicily and the subsequent Allied invasion of Italy in 1943. It was also used to provide aerial support at D-Day and the Normandy Landings in 1944. Towards the end of the war in the Pacific it became part of the aerial component of the British Pacific Fleet, used off the coast of Japan in the war's final days.

Kittie Perry was an air mechanic with the WRNS (Women's Royal Naval Service, nicknamed the Wrens) working on Seafire engines from 1942 to 1945. When she joined the Wrens she was twenty and living with her family in London. 'My father was a marine engineer so I had more or less grown up between a screwdriver and a hammer. I had two older brothers, one went into the Army, one into the Navy and the Fleet Air Arm, so I decided to volunteer for the Wrens.'

Two weeks of basic training in London, mostly learning about the Navy, were followed by categorization. 'The categories we were put in depended on what was needed at the time and they needed air mechanics to replace the men who were going overseas. You can guess how they felt when they saw a load of Wrens about to take their jobs!

'I was deemed to be an engine mechanic. I went on a six-month training course in Stafford, trained by Petty and Chief Petty Officers, most of whom had had a rough time at sea.' (Petty Officer is a non-commissioned rank in the Navy, a supervisory role equivalent to a Flight Sergeant in the RAF.) 'This was supposed to be a light job for them. But I don't think they found it like that. Imagine it: a load of young girls around the same age, early twenties, many of whom had never seen a hammer or a screwdriver in their life, all there to be trained. One of the girls lived in the heart of London's West End. She'd never done anything remotely practical in her life.

'We were given a toolbox full of tools and for the first couple of weeks you learned what these different things were for. Not many of us dropped out at the end of the six months. We had exams every two weeks and if you failed, you were sent down a class. No one wanted that because you'd made friends by then.'

After training, the girls were sent off to various coastal naval air stations. 'I was now an engine mechanic and I was sent off to RNAS Donibristle, a Fleet Air Arm base north-west of Edinburgh. We wore navy serge bell bottoms, navy blue shirts, black lace-ups, navy jacket or skirt. And the round hats with HMS [His Majesty's Ship] on the front. I worked on Seafires (known to us as Spits). A number of aircraft were built purely for the Navy, including the Barracudas, the Walrus, the Hurricanes and some American aircraft.

'The Seafires went onto the naval carriers to be catapulted off and landed on the sea. Donibristle was a maintenance station. Rosyth was nearby and that was a naval base. HMS *Implacable*, a naval air carrier, was docked at Rosyth. They'd fly off a pack of Seafires or whatever else they had on board to Donibristle for engine changes or general inspections, and afterwards they'd be flown back to Rosyth, ready for action. The Spits were very light aircraft, very closely fitted in the cockpit. Prior to that there was the Swordfish, which had an open cockpit. But the Seafire had a tendency, when you were testing the engine, if you took it up over a certain strength with the throttle, for its tail to wave – so you lay in the slipstream with your back to the pilot and you just had to stay there while he tested.

'Lying on it was not all that wonderful – your hair was blown on end. We used to give each other home perms, and then the wind would blow it and make it awful – so tangled you couldn't get a brush or comb through it.'

There were also daily engine inspections, which meant draining all the oil out of the oil sump into a drum, ready to put clean oil in. 'That was dirty work,' Kittie recalled. 'On one occasion, the Petty Officer who was in charge said to me: "Go to the stores and ask for a long weight." I didn't know what that was for, or even what it looked like and at the stores the chap behind the hatch walked away after I'd asked for it.'

Kittie waited there for half an hour. 'Then he came back. "Er … what was it you wanted?" "A long weight," I replied. "Well, you've had one now, haven't you?" The whole thing was a big joke, a bit of fun for the men. The Petty Officer and the guy in the store had set me up!'

There was more entertainment for the men when Kittie was taking an engine to pieces and needed a supply of locking wire. 'On the aircraft, for every screw that had a nut on it, there was a locking nut. But because of the vibration of the engine when it was running continuously, it would work loose. Every nut had a tiny hole in it. You had locking wire to put through the hole and lock the nut onto the screw, so it would not work loose. You'd go to the stores to the open hatch and ask for locking wire. He'd have it hanging up.

"Oh, just pull what you want," the guy said. Those strands of wire were about two feet long and he'd have the other end attached to a megger [an insulation resistance tester] with a handle. That created a current, so as you pulled one of these wires, he'd turn the handle and you'd get an electric shock. Another joke to play on us.'

But the girls working alongside Kittie knew how to get their own back. 'One of the girls shouted "Oh no, my watch has come off in the oil drum," so the Petty Officer had to take off his jacket, roll up his sleeve ready to put his hand in the drum to retrieve it. A very dirty prospect. Then, just before he did it, we'd tell him: "ONLY JOKING!" That was *our* joke.'

There were other dirty jobs, especially refuelling the Spits. 'You'd have to check the level in the cockpit and top it up to the full amount. But first you'd have to find the aircraft. They were picketed [parked] all over the field, scattered everywhere. So they'd hand you a number like a car registration and you'd go off to find it with your list of instructions – a number of checks you had to do including the refuelling. To refuel, you had to look out for a bowser [a mobile tank], which would be driven very slowly round the area all the time. Then you'd have to direct it back to the plane you were working on. The bowsers were driven by civilian drivers. They'd drive up to the plane you were working on, hand you the nozzle and then climb back into the bowser so you could fill the Spit up. The Spit was very low to the ground and the hole of the petrol tank was just above the wing.

'It meant lying on the wing holding this nozzle. It was

heavy work. It would take us two thumbs to release the cap, the nozzle would go into the hole – as you would with a car – then you'd shout "Okay!" to the driver of the bowser and he'd release his tap. But you needed massive strength to release the cap. Also, the fuel gauge was in the cockpit and you were lying on the wing, so you didn't know it was full until the petrol spilled out. And where did it go? All over your button-up overalls! You'd be filthy,' recalls Kittie. 'And you didn't dare go near anyone with a match for their ciggie!'

There were men doing the same job as Kittie, but when it came to certain tasks, only the women were told to do them. 'Battle of Britain Spits had white stripes painted on their wings. If they came through our hands at Donibristle they had to be scrubbed off. None of the men were told to scrub them off, only the women. We'd all had exactly the same training, mind you. But the men weren't told to scrub.'

Kittie and a friend decided to make a formal complaint about this. 'If you had a complaint, you lined up at 9 a.m. and stood outside the office door. Two of us went into the lieutenant and made our objection. His response was: "If I wanted you to scrub my floor here, you'd scrub it!" Within days, word had got round that we were "rebels". Then, out of the blue, my friend was transferred 50 miles up the coast.'

Kittie remembered her time working on the Seafires with a certain amount of pride. 'The work we did, no matter how small it was in the scale of things, mattered. You were still part of all the activity.' Kittie died in April 2017, aged ninety-five.

## The Squadron Dog

Since the earliest days of aviation, the squadron or hangar dog has retained a very special place in the combat pilot's life. In the midst of the strong camaraderie and bravado of the Battle of Britain fighter squadrons, the four-legged friend is seen frequently in the airfield images of those crucial months in the summer of 1940 when Britain's future hung in the balance.

It isn't difficult to understand why squadron dogs were so important for the morale of the young pilots: young men love dogs, and dogs return affection in never ending measure. In addition, at a time of extreme stress and ragged nerves – and sometimes sudden personal loss – the squadron dog provided comfort and momentary release from care, a link to normality. In fact, some squadrons valued their canine companions so much, they made moves to include their dogs on a formal basis.

One example of this is 152 Squadron at Warmwell in south-west Dorset. The pilots of the squadron listed their dog as 'Pilot Officer Pooch'; Pooch even had his own allocation of rations.

Visitors to the Battle of Britain memorial site at Capel le Ferne in Kent can see a permanent acknowledgement of the importance of squadron dogs in the bronze sculpture entitled 'B. O. B., The Squadron Dog'. The sculpture was commissioned back in 1995 and, at the time, it was decided the dog should be a Labrador. Nowadays, so lifelike is the sculpture, visitors have been known to put down water for the Battle of Britain dog.

One of the better known canine companions of the Battle of Britain pilots is Wing Commander George 'Grumpy' Unwin's pet Alsatian, Flash, the Spitfire pilot's steadfast and loyal companion who virtually became 19 Squadron's mascot at RAF Duxford that summer in 1940. (Legend has it that Unwin's nickname of 'Grumpy' was given to him after he repeatedly complained about not being allocated an aircraft during the Dunkirk crisis. Another story claims he earned the nickname from fighter pilot Douglas Bader, based at Duxford at the time. One night, Bader was noisily adjusting his artificial legs when Unwin told him to be quiet. 'Shut up, Grumpy,' Bader is reputed to have replied.)

George Unwin was a miner's son who joined the RAF in a clerical job, volunteered to be a pilot in 1935 and was one of the first ever Spitfire fighter pilots with 19 Squadron, the first RAF squadron to take delivery of the Spitfire. By the end of his many Battle of Britain Spitfire sorties from Duxford in 1940 he was credited with having shot down 14 enemy aircraft. During his time as a pilot he was awarded the Distinguished Service Order (DSO) and the Distinguished Flying Medal (DFM) and Bar. He left the RAF in 1961 as a Wing Commander and died in June 2006, aged ninety-three.

## Life with the Clickety Click Squadron

Corporal Bob Morris joined the RAF before the Second World War. He was studying aeronautical engineering at the RAF Technical School at Halton, Buckinghamshire, an apprentice training to be a Fitter IIE (engines) when war broke out. 'Because of the urgent need for more personnel thereafter, activities such as time off and sport were cancelled to get us trained quickly. In May 1940, I passed out as an Airman 1st Class and discovered that I was posted to 66 Squadron at RAF Coltishall.' 'Clickety click' was a rhyming slang term (used in bingo or 'housey-housey' games) for the number 66, and 66 Squadron was often referred to by this name.

'I knew neither the location of Coltishall or what aircraft 66 Squadron had. Coltishall was in Norfolk, and my first glimpse of 66 Squadron was from the bus travelling alongside the airfield for a short distance – what a thrill to see Spitfires! This was a young man's dream! In 66 Squadron I found the set-up was that there were two groups of technical people who looked after the aircraft. The trades in the RAF were sub-divided into five, the technical people being in the first, and we did all the major work on the aircraft.

'Group two were flight mechanics, the semi-skilled, and their job was to look after the aircraft's daily requirements, like the daily inspection: oil, petrol, tyre pressures, etc. In our group there was a Fitter Engines and a Fitter Airframe, likewise in the second there was a Flight Mechanic Engine and a Flight Mechanic Airframe. The latter two always remained with the same aircraft. The Flight Mechanic Engine would start up the aircraft's engine first thing in the morning, so that when a scramble call came the engine was already nice and warm. We Fitter IIEs, however, never had an aircraft of our own as there were less of us, so we could be called upon to work on any of the squadron's Spitfires.

We used to do the 30-, 60- and 90-hour inspections. When each aircraft had done the maximum amount of flying hours per its particular type of engine, it had an engine change – we would also do those.

'My first jobs were mainly inspections, as opposed to repair work. I remember a pilot getting into the cockpit and I helped him get going, pulled the chocks away and set him up to fly. As he taxied out I thought to myself, "I'll bet he doesn't know that this is my first attempt!" Perhaps he wouldn't have taken off so confidently had he known!

'We shared Coltishall with the Hurricanes of 242 Squadron, but we were not there for long as we were moved to Kenley in 11 Group, right down in the thick of it, the Battle of Britain having started by this time. When we arrived at Kenley on 3 September 1940, it was an absolute shambles. There was hardly a building left standing. As we drove around the aerodrome to our assembly point, I saw a car park full of vehicles – but there was not one which hadn't been riddled by gunfire or shrapnel. There were shelters destroyed, buildings flattened. We were only at Kenley for a week, but that short time was absolutely devastating. During that week I think we lost eight pilots, so at the end of it we were practically out of action.

'From a ground viewpoint we had to learn very quickly about air raids which were incoming thick and fast. Once I looked up and saw five parachutes descending. We were now dispersed around the edge of the airfield with plenty of space between each aircraft. We could not put the aircraft either in a hangar or in a group for fear of them being wiped out altogether. However, it meant that we had to work on them out in the open, often without any cover when a raid occurred. They had built some blast pens at Kenley, but nowhere near enough, so you could be a quarter of a mile away from any shelter. It is perhaps surprising but you do get used to it, almost blasé about it, in fact.

'We used to carry on working after the siren had gone, right up until the Germans were practically overhead. If you then left your aircraft and lay down on the ground some distance away from it, the chances of being killed by a bomb were remote. Strafing was a bit more hazardous, but the greatest problem was bomb-blast, i.e. what it actually threw in the air. If it exploded near a road, building or runway then huge chunks of concrete and masonry could come falling down on you. You therefore tended to lie there and keep your fingers crossed that when all the rubbish thrown up came down, none of it hit you.

'On 10 September 1940, 66 Squadron moved to Gravesend which was no more than a civilian flying club airfield. We were the only squadron there, at what was Biggin Hill's satellite. At Gravesend we looked down on the River Thames, opposite Tilbury, and I remember bombs hitting large floating oil tanks in the river there. I always admired the sailors of the little boats, tugs and the like, that used to pull out those tanks which were on fire, to stop the flames spreading. However, we were not bombed at Gravesend.

'There was only one hangar there, our dining room, a small hut for flying control and a pilots' crew room, and that was it. Without much to hit on a grass airfield, we would have been hard to put out of action anyway.

'By this time though,' Bob recalls, 'we were finding the living conditions at Gravesend a bit trying. We had a half day off every ten days. We used to spend that half day fast asleep. We were exhausted working such long hours, from dawn to dusk. At Gravesend there were no billets, so a restaurant about three quarters of a mile away, called 'Laughing Waters', adjacent to a big lake, was commandeered. We were taken there in our usual mode of motorized transport – a Bedford three-tonner. The building was just a shell, nothing on the floor and all we had to sleep in was two blankets. It was a mighty cold place with just two blankets and the floor, on the edge of a lake! The only thing that had not been taken away were the rowing boats, so every morning to get warm we rowed around the lake.

'Fortunately, we were not in Laughing Waters for very long before they decided to move our billets again, this time to Cobham Hall, the Earl of Darnley's estate. We slept in the servants' quarters, but at least we had beds. We were quite near Cobham village and it was strange. Wherever we were the officers would find a restaurant or similar for their evening drinks whilst we other ranks would find a pub or similar. We never went into their places and they never into ours.

'As we had lost so many pilots at Kenley, we now had replacements arriving at Gravesend, although we still lost several more pilots at Gravesend. However, one of the young pilots that got killed there I had actually got to know quite well – Pilot Officer Reilley. He was an American who got into the RAF through a Canadian connection as, of course, the USA was still neutral at this time. He was just twenty-two when he was shot down and killed over Westerham in Kent on 17 October. By this time we were quite accustomed to losses. It sounds terrible to say that now, but I think you can get used to anything.

'I was on my half day, fast asleep on my bed at Cobham Hall as we usually were on our half days off, when the Sergeant stuck his head round the door and said: "Everybody on half day – outside, best blue, best greatcoat, webbing belt round your waist and get on the lorry!" He did not tell us what for but we got dressed and piled into the lorry – it took us to a church near Gravesend, and it was then that we realized we were going to be Guard of Honour at Pilot Officer Reilley's funeral. As he was from overseas, there were no family there, but we sat in the church for the service.

'A four-wheel trailer was hitched up to our truck and the coffin was put on this trailer. We had to march behind it through the middle of Gravesend to the cemetery where the burial took place. Afterwards we piled on the lorry to go back to Cobham Hall. On the way back someone said that since he had arrived in the UK, Reilley had got married and his wife had recently given birth to a little baby boy. In 1983 I attended a 66 Squadron reunion at Kenley – there I met a man in his forties, a family man, who was Reilley's son!

'At Gravesend we got a new CO – Squadron Leader Athol Forbes replaced Rupert Leigh, and we lost Pilot Officers Mather and Corbett, and Flight Lieutenant Gillies. I remember being at Gravesend on what was considered at the time to have been the great day – 15 September 1940 – now celebrated as Battle of Britain Day. At Gravesend we used to watch the German aircraft coming in, heading for London or elsewhere, the trails in the sky, and how relieved we were when they passed overhead and went straight on! During that September, as we were so close to the river, there would often be a ground mist which lasted all day. You may have a day with absolute thick fog in which no aircraft could take off, or no bombing could take place because the Germans could not see us. We used to get all our work done by early afternoon and then, inevitably, a football always seemed to appear from somewhere, and a game would start on the edge of the aerodrome.

'We never used to pick a side, you just joined in with whichever side appeared to be winning and that was the way you kicked! On one occasion we were busy playing in thick fog – you could only see about half-way across the airfield – when we heard these German aircraft circling round above us looking for something to bomb. Suddenly, right through the fog came a parachute flare which landed on our football pitch – someone kicked some dirt onto it and we just kept on playing – the Germans then flew off. No one ran for shelter. That was how used we had become to it all. You never heard anyone talk about defeat. Of course, we were not conversant with all the facts, though occasionally we would get some air force bigwig come down and give us all a pep talk.

'It was towards the end of our time at Gravesend that we began to see the DFCs and DFMs being awarded to the pilots. And, of course, I remember the aircraft damaged in combat. I remember Pilot Officer "Bogle" Bodie coming back with his port mainplane knocked about by a cannon shell and I had to rip part of the aileron off for him which he proudly took as a souvenir. I always remember a Spitfire coming in making a horrible whistling noise – it had a bullet hole right through a propeller blade! We did not have a new propeller, however, so we smoothed out the hole and drilled corresponding holes in the other two blades – it then flew for another fortnight with that same airscrew! We had to drill the other holes as when the propeller is assembled it is very finely balanced to prevent vibration.

'Sixty-six Squadron must have been about the first squadron to fly a clipped-wing Spitfire. That was at Kenley and by accident – a Spitfire came in with a badly mangled wing-tip and other damage, so it had to go back to the maintenance depot as it could not be repaired by the squadron. We took off the damaged wing-tip, put doped canvas on the square-ended wing-tip as it now was, and did likewise with the other wing. The aircraft flew back to the depot as a clipped-wing Spitfire, the actual official modification not coming out, of course, until 1942.

'On 30 October 1940 we moved from Gravesend to West Malling, although I could never understand why they moved us such short distances. A squadron move is a very complicated business involving a great deal of men, engineering equipment and spares. West Malling is about two minutes' flying time from Gravesend, so I could never understand the logic behind moving the squadron there, about 12 to 15 miles. Someone said that it was to confuse the enemy – it certainly confused us! We were there no more than a couple of weeks before abandoning West Malling as the airfield was like a bog – the aircraft would land and then sink up to their axles in mud. We were then moved to Biggin Hill on 7 November. Upon arrival we found that station to be a shambles, too. There were very few buildings still standing. There were no billets etc., so the military commandeered a Women's Institute hall – no beds, nothing – we were given white linen sacks. A farmer gave us a load of straw, so we filled up our sacks with straw. You just walked in, found a little bit of empty floor, plonked it down with your two blankets, and that was where you lived.

'Our washing facilities were fire buckets. The only time you had hot water was when a fire bucket was heated over the stove. Because of the conditions under which we were working and living, we were getting very tired. You can stick this kind of thing for a while, but soon enough the strain begins to tell. However, we soldiered on.

'So far as the aerodrome was concerned, it was another hard slog. No buildings to work in, so again we were always working out in the open. We were sharing the aerodrome with 94 and 74 Squadrons. Once again it was a case of scrambles, sirens telling us to take shelter, carry on working, inspection procedures, just the hard unromantic slog.

'We did have some raids and bombs dropped but what can you say about it?' Bob said. 'One raid in the end tends to be just a repetition of the last. I saw some dogfights over Biggin Hill. Once when we were in an aircraft bay we saw a German aircraft on fire, and four parachutes come out, two of which were on fire. We saw these two German aircrew falling faster and faster until the parachutes had completely burnt away and they fell to their deaths. Although you knew that enemy aircraft were being shot down, you rarely saw one as they were collected regularly by the Maintenance

Units. At Biggin Hill, however, I had the chance to look over a Me 109 which was on the station and virtually complete. I looked in the cockpit and it was nowhere near the Spitfire's instrumentation standards – it was very bleak.

'On 24 February 1941, we moved from Biggin Hill and left 11 Group to join 10 Group at Exeter. From Exeter we provided protection for the docks at Plymouth and Bristol; 504 Squadron's Hurricanes were also at Exeter. We were still well within the action. Again, no billets so a house was commandeered for us to live in. Because we were living outside the camp, we devised a system whereby a team of us fitters would take it in turns to sleep on the aerodrome, in a wooden hut, every third night. The German bombers still paid us a visit. It happened when we were sleeping in the wooden hut, we were bombed quite heavily. The Sergeant in charge and myself got out of the hut, but as there was no shelter we jumped down into a ditch which had running water. We got into it and crouched down with bombs and incendiaries showering down all around us. It was quite frightening. It is strange but by the note of a bomb's whistle you can accurately estimate the distance from you it is going to hit. Eventually, we heard one coming down and the Sergeant shouted "Heads down! This is ours!"

'It was close enough – the next morning I measured from where I was to the edge of the crater and it was only twenty-five to thirty feet [7.62–9.144 m]. We had been showered in rubble and mortar, and the bomb blocked up the stream so that the water started rising and we had to get out. Our hut had completely collapsed. We had to find somewhere else to shelter, but the problem with negotiating an unlit airfield at night is that there are many obstacles in the shape of equipment left lying about, like hand-pulled oil bowsers [tankers] and racks of oxygen bottles. Fortunately, the bombers soon disappeared, and we went around putting incendiaries out, using the sand that had been left in piles at various locations on the airfield. Unfortunately, they had not put any anti-freeze in with the sand so at first the tumps [mounds] were frozen solid! I spent the next couple of hours with a big piece of timber breaking up the sand whilst others rushed around with spadefuls. Several aircraft were damaged on the ground. By morning it was obvious that as a squadron we were going to be non-operational for a while. I remember going back and looking at where I had been crouched in the ditch and around that position there were about a dozen incendiaries sticking out of the ground, and some in the water even closer to where I had been. If one of those hit you, you would have been dead. We got them all out before being relieved by the daylight shift.

'Shortly after this they moved us to a billet on the aerodrome. If the night bombers came over we would get under our beds, which was also protection if the hut came down on top of you. One night it was quite moonlit and I went outside to see the German bombers going over. Incendiaries had been dropped and there were fires everywhere. We ran down to see what we could do. There was a Wellington that had landed for an overnight stop and it was well alight. We had to go close to it when we were running to help our own squadron, but an officer shouted at us to get some fire extinguishers. We had to do what he said so we got a couple of hand-held extinguishers and this officer had us standing in front of this Wellington, which was blazing madly all over, squirting two hand-held fire extinguishers onto it! The silly sod stood there guiding us where to squirt them – frankly it was like peeing in the Thames to raise the water level! At the same time there was .303 ammunition going off from the aircraft's machine-guns, and we did not know whether there were any bombs on board. This daft so and so just hadn't got a clue.

'Soon the extinguishers ran out, so he ordered us off to get some more, so off we went – we knew he didn't know who we were because he was not one of our officers, so once we got out of sight we just carried on to our own squadron. There we had the job of putting out incendiaries which had also started a lot of fires on the headquarters' brick buildings. As the firemen were committed there, we had to look after ourselves. We later went up to the cookhouse to see if there was any cocoa going, filled our mugs full and went back to our billets to sleep. Next morning we were working flat out again. Strangely, all the nights we were bombed, 504 Squadron was always untouched.

'On another night we were bombed again. As we ran for cover a friend of mine tripped straight over a bomb that was half sticking out of the ground! He just picked himself up and carried on whilst I gave it a very wide berth!

'One morning our pilots were supposed to be on stand-by, but did not arrive at dispersal by the appointed hour. Sixty-six Squadron was then sent to Perranporth in Cornwall as a punishment. We were right on the cliffs – when the Spitfires took off they were almost over the sea. Again there were no billets so we lived at the Atlantic

Hotel but again there was no furniture, so it was back to the floor. Ginger Finch and I found a little place nearby that did bed and breakfast, so we stayed there one night – what a treat to sleep in a real bed!'

Whilst at Perranporth, Bob's time with 66 Squadron came to an end and he was posted overseas. 'By and large, we ground crew were all quite young. I was nineteen and the pilots were often only in their early twenties. Being young was an advantage because you're not so aware of the dangers. Looking back, I think that I would be much more frightened if I had to do it all again. Being young, you tended to take it all so much more lightly. But I look back on those times with great pride and affection.'

After the war, Bob left the RAF and worked for many years as an engineer. He retired in 1986 and died on 29 November 2014, aged ninety-two, in Shobdon, Herefordshire.

## Doping the Walrus

R. J. Mitchell designed many other aircraft after the Spitfire before his death in 1937. One of these was the Walrus, a single-engine amphibian biplane that initially operated as a fleet spotter to be launched from battleships.

Increasingly, however, the Walrus was used as a rescue aircraft for downed aircrew during the war, a distant cousin of the Spitfire certainly, but no less effective as part of the war effort. Operated by the Fleet Air Arm, the Walrus also served with the RAF, the Royal Australian Airforce and the Royal New Zealand Airforce.

Two variants of the Walrus, the Mark I and Mark II, were manufactured by marine engineering company Saunders-Roe (or Saro) at Cowes, Isle of Wight, during the war years when many women, like Annie Bridges, from Newport, were employed in the company's factories in a variety of munitions jobs. (From early 1941 it was compulsory for women aged between eighteen and sixty to register for war work. Any woman who was pregnant or had a child under fourteen was not required to register – but, like Annie, they could volunteer.)

In 1941, Annie was twenty-one, married and had one young child when she started working at Saunders-Roe as a cleaner. Part of her work involved cleaning out the Walrus biplanes after they'd returned from rescue operations. 'I had mostly worked as a cleaner ever since I left school, for the simple reason that in those days, that was all that was available. That, and a little bit of shop work.

'I left school at fourteen, so at one stage I did two jobs: cleaning houses and working in a little general shop called Perkins. Later on, I found work in Woolworth's – one pound, nineteen shillings and sixpence a week. That was the best paid work on the island in those days. But after war broke out, factory work was a better bet: more than two pounds a week. And at Woolworth's, after I got married, they wanted me to do supervisor work, bossing people about, I didn't want to do that.

'I went to Saunders-Roe by choice. It was munitions work but it was the best money I could get. And my sister already worked there. She worked in what they called doping. [Aircraft dope was a glue-like varnish, a plasticized lacquer applied to fabric-covered aircraft: the wings of the Walrus were covered in fabric. The dope tightened and stiffened the fabric stretched over the wings, making them weatherproof. The job of painting the dope onto the fabric was quite dangerous, because the fumes from the varnish could be toxic.] We worked in separate factories – hers was at one end of Forest Road, where they did the doping and the painting of the planes, mine was at the other end, where all the cleaning of the planes was done.

'It was all women working where I worked, with just one man in charge of us all. The women had to do it, didn't they, because the men had all been called up. I had women of all ages working alongside me. Some were very old, even retired. We'd start work at 8.30 a.m. and go straight to the bench where we'd sit, cleaning the screws or getting underneath the aircraft and cleaning it, then getting inside it and cleaning it out. You'd work all day long till five o'clock, six days a week. You didn't work Sundays. They were working all the time in the factory, so there were night shifts, too, but I wasn't interested in night work.

'We didn't have a canteen, so we used to take our own lunch. It was harder work than I'd known before but, as I say, the pay was better. There was no uniform as such, you just wore an overall. No training either. When you started, they just gave you a can of cleaning stuff, a brush and let you get on with it.

'The work was repetitive, the same thing day after day, but it was good fun because the women I worked with were a good crowd. In my section there'd have been about twenty-five of us and we helped each other because we were more or less doing the same thing, cleaning the screws and the bodies of the aeroplanes.

'It was a good work atmosphere but it was bloomin' cold, freezing in the winter – we had no heating. With those big hangar doors open all the time it was terrible. Once they even sent us home it was so cold and our hair was white with frost! But you got on with it. It was war and that was it.

'My sister joined a union. If you worked in the doping and painting factory you could do that but the cleaners were not allowed to have any union. We didn't really have a trade. I mean anyone could clean screws.

'After D-Day there was a heck of a lot of work to be done 'cos those planes were in the water for a long time before we got them back, so you can imagine the state they were in. One day I found a coin in a plane I was cleaning out. It was a ha'penny, an old ha'penny, and I often wondered what happened to that person, because those sea planes were used to rescue people, like ambulances in a way, bringing home the injured. They'd remove all the seats in the planes in order to make them more like ambulances. I've still got that ha'penny.

'Of course, at work there were air raid warnings all the time, but we never bothered much about those warnings. We just had one lady that worked with us that used to get under the table while the air raid was on until the all clear went but the rest of us just used to carry on working. We had no shelters to run to, anyway. Our factory wasn't bombed; there were places not far away that suffered bomb damage. But that was at night.

'The worst thing for us was lack of money for everything – lack of coupons for clothes. My husband was away, so we only got what the Army gave us. Which wasn't much. You were so hard up then. I lived with an aunt and she looked after my daughter for me. I wouldn't have been able to go to work if not for that. But a lot of us lived that way. There were a lot of other women just like me. You had to be resourceful and learn to adapt. Meat was short, butter and sugar were short, but you just learned to go without.

'But I do think the Second World War liberated women for the simple reason that we had to do so much more than we normally would've done. I was quite happy with my lot, really. I don't think I could've done anything different. You got on with it. And that was it.'

Annie Bridges died on 24 October 2012, aged ninety-three.

## A Poem for Ground Crew

The ground crew servicing the Spitfires or, to use the RAF slang term, the 'erks' (from the Cockney pronunciation of the world 'aircraft') were the backroom boys of the squadron. It was their job to ensure the planes were in good working order, to get them back up with full power following a sortie and, in many cases, to work round the clock so that the pilots could take to the skies swiftly. There were three main roles for the ground crew: the fitter, who was the engine specialist, responsible for maintaining the engine and engine controls; the rigger, responsible for the airframe structure, flying controls, hydraulic systems, landing gear and transparencies; and the armourers, responsible for providing the fire power for the aircraft, preparing the bombs, and ensuring fresh supplies of ammunition were ready to take onboard. These tradesmen were a special breed, as many fighter pilots came to understand. They worked in tough conditions, especially when overseas, but they were as dedicated to their work as any fighter pilot or those of senior rank.

At the start of the Second World War, there were certain class distinctions between the flyers and the servicemen, mostly because that was the way life ran at the time, the 'everyone in their place' theme of the British classbound society of the 1930s. But this slowly started to change during the Second World War, as people were often thrown together, through necessity, with men or women they might not have ordinarily met in peacetime. The bond between the 'erk' and the pilot grew, both fully acknowledging the importance of each other's role, and it became a close working relationship.

This poem, dated 1944, and credited to RAF Flying Officer Jack Brittain (Vernon Brittain Gray) conveys a great deal about this relationship. After the war, in 1955, Gray became a commissioned Flight Lieutenant. He retired from the RAF in 1971 and died in 1976.

*Ain't feeling quite so good today, I'm even off me beer!*
*Although they've given me ten days leave I still feel kinda queer,*
*I've had a nasty shock, you see, I've lost my biggest chum*
*It happened just a week ago, and better men don't come.*

*My pal's a famous fighter ace, DSO and DFC*
*His score of Jerry buses had just reached twenty-three,*
*Squadron Leader Brand\* the finest bloke I've met*
*Him and me was really pals, that makes you smile I bet.*

*Him a proper English gent, public school and Oxford Blue*
*And me a common Cockney bloke, just an AC2.*
*A Spitfire fighter pilot and his rigger, that was us*
*The bloke who did the scrapping and me who did his bus.*

*'A fighting team' he said we were, although he'd got three rings.*
*'Jimmy you're all right' he said, although he'd got the wings.*
*'You're the bloke that I depend on when I'm up there in a fight,*
*'I can't shoot 'em down unless you fix my Spitfire right.'*

*He was always kind and thoughtful, when my missus had a kid*
*He sent a wire, a bunch of flowers as well as fifteen quid.*
*I told him I was grateful, said I'd make it up to him.*
*He gave a crooked smile and said: 'You owe me nothing, Jim.*

*I've got a pair of silver Wings, two medals on my chest,*
*My name's been in the papers, there's promotion and the rest.*
*I've got twenty-three swastikas painted on my petrol tank*
*For all these things it's blokes like you I've really got to thank.'*

*The day he'd been to see the King to get his DSO*
*They 'ad a lovely party, all 'is friends and the CO.*
*But 'e got away for just a while to buy us drinks all round.*
*'You can't win medals in the sky with dud blokes on the ground.'*

*'Killer' Brand they called him, the pilot of no Wing,*
*What a name to give a bloke who'd never harm a thing,*
*Except when he was chasing Huns; Blimey then he'd fight!*
*You see he lost his sister when Jerry came one night.*

*The girls were crazy after him, they chased him near and far,*
*Made his life a misery, just like a movie star.*
*Wouldn't have no truck with 'em, perhaps they thought him*
*   dumb,*
*If they did, he didn't worry, his best girl was his mum.*

*A week ago last Monday, I won't forget that day,*
*It was cold and wet and dreary, all the sky was grey.*
*They took off them twelve Spitfires on an early morning sweep.*
*Just like a hundred other days, I waved and said 'God keep'.*

*I couldn't seem to settle down the time they was away,*
*I seemed to have a feeling this was going to be his day.*
*I waited on the airfield 'til I sighted them – and then,*
*One, two, three, four, five, six, seven, eight, nine, ten.*

*I quickly checked them over but his crate it wasn't there.*
*I asked the other pilots if they'd seen him bail and where?*
*They'd seen him crashing down in flames, 'He's gone, we fear'.*
*I ain't feeling quite so good today – I'm even off me beer!*

* a pseudonym, as is the nickname 'Killer' Brand and 'Jim'.


## The Armourer's Story

Fred Roberts' first RAF posting was to 19 Squadron at
Duxford, the first fighter squadron to receive Spitfires.
Arming and re-arming the planes at the beginning of the
Second World War proved to be a learning curve for Fred
and the ground teams as they worked on the early Spitfires
during those tumultuous months of the Battle of Britain.

Fred was eighteen when he signed up for the RAF in Swansea. Until then, he'd been in the tinplate industry, rolling tin plates. His meagre pay helped support his family but Fred wanted a trade. So he signed up for seven years as an armourer. One year on, his training completed, he was an AC2 (Aircraftman Class 2 Armourer). It was July 1939 when Fred was posted to No 19 (Fighter) Squadron at Duxford. 'After parade, the morning after we arrived, we were marched to the armoury. We were told to walk around the hangar with the lads and familiarize ourselves with the Spitfire. I still remember the thrill, the first time I sat in the cockpit of that Spitfire and had the control column in my hand. Of all the hundreds of times I sat in Spitfires in later years, it was never like that first time.

'Another thing that greeted us in the armoury was the clothes line, complete with feminine underwear, brassieres, knickers, etc. These, we were told, were the spoils of war; no sexual victories were to be boasted about unless accompanied with a trophy. But we found out later in the morning that the trophies were really salvaged from the rags issued from the stores for gun cleaning and were hung as decorations in an otherwise dreary room.

'The tool kit I was issued with consisted of a wooden box eighteen inches square and ten inches deep (lockable if one had some keys), a pair of six-inch pliers, an eight-inch screwdriver, an oil can and two BA spanners.

'Despite the claims of lots of people that we used our Field Service caps to cock the Browning machine guns, I never heard of this or saw it happen. We would have had to buy a new cap if we had damaged ours in any way. We all had a cocking toggle that we made with a piece of thick fence wire and a three-inch piece of broom handle. This we were never without when on duty. Another invaluable tool was a round of .303 ball or armour piercing ammunition. The point of the bullet was the best tool to remove and replace the breech block return spring of a Browning gun.'

Harmonizing the Spitfire's guns was part of the job. 'We used to take the Spitfire down to the firing range at Duxford, put it up on trestles, level it fore and aft and laterally and then sight the guns. We had a target in front of the firing range and we sighted the guns on the target and the gun sight was harmonized with the guns. Then we got the pilot along and he went along all the guns. We had a little microscope that we put on the breach of the guns to sight them and he went along on the wing to make certain that the guns were sighted on the target and to his satisfaction – the same with the gun sight. Then we locked all the guns, wired and blocked them up. They did change that after Dunkirk. A lot of pilots disagreed with this method of sighting and they had their guns harmonized on a dartboard type target, about 300 yards in front of the Spitfire, and all eight guns were harmonized on this one central point.

'Charlie Stanley [Stan], who had first introduced me to Spitfires, had sort of taken me under his wing and we became great friends. We became a team, working together, making our daily inspection and other maintenance work easier. Stan had been with 19 Squadron when they had Gloster Gauntlets, and so had been working with Spits from the start.'

There was much to be learned. For a start, there was the jargon. 'Anything that flew was a kite, not a Spit or a

Hurricane or a Wellington and when the word "DOORS" was shouted by "A" or "B" Flight Chiefy, one didn't look around to see where it was – everyone within hearing immediately found somewhere to hide; in a cockpit, under benches, behind trestles, anywhere, as the call meant hard work pushing open or closing the hangar doors. No easy job on the old Duxford hangar doors! "Two to six" was the shout to push when sufficient bodies had been conscripted to do the job and was also the call to lift, when lifting an aircraft onto trestles, or any physical work requiring more than two of us.'

There was also the task of pushing the aircraft in and out of the hangar daily, daily inspections to be carried out and serviceability forms to be signed. 'I was expected to assist the Flight Mechanics, Engine and Airframe, to start up the aircraft by connecting up the accumulator starter trolley, pressing the button on the signal from the cockpit and disconnecting the cable from the engine after starting, taking care not to walk into the spinning propeller while doing so. I was also expected to lend my body weight to the tail plane while the flight mechanic or pilot revved up the engine and blew my head off, or so it seemed. As part of the team on a particular aircraft I also assisted in steadying the aircraft while it was being taxied over the grass area by holding the wing tip. There were also times when I was required to pull the wheel chocks away on the pilot's request. All duties we were never taught at armament school.'

War was now imminent. On 24 August 1939, all leave was stopped and personnel on leave were recalled. 'We all knew there was a possibility of war against Germany, but none of us thought it was really so serious. On 2 September and immediately after my Daily Inspection duties, three other armament staff and I were sent along to Whittlesford railway station. There we found seven or eight rail wagons, all full of .303 ammunition waiting to be unloaded and transported to the ammunition dump at Duxford. Two or three days' work.

'I can still see the trains travelling through the station, passing us frequently, full of evacuee children and their school teachers, all from London, travelling to Norfolk, waving madly. On Sunday, 3 September, we were back at the station again to carry on with the unloading. More evacuee trains passing through. At 1100 hrs, the landlord of the Railway Tavern, adjacent to the goods yard, invited us all into his back room and drew us all a pint of his best ale, gratis. We listened together to the radio and Chamberlain's speech declaring war on Germany. Shortly after this, the local air raid sirens were screaming and from the station yard we saw 19 and 66 Squadron aircraft take off and circle around before landing again. One of the lads said: "I don't know what good they can do except ram any Germans, there's no ammo in them Spitfires. We've got it all here!"

'The transporting of the ammo complete, I was one of a party making up the ammo into belts of three-hundred rounds each for a couple of days. They contained ball, armour piercing, incendiary and tracer. Around this time, a bit of a mystery: a young ex-apprentice armourer working with us chalked slogans outside and inside our little ammo room. They were all in German. Then, after a few days, he disappeared with no word or explanation to anyone. We never saw him again.

'Now all of us armourers and assistants were practising re-arming for hours every day until two armourers and two assistants could change all of a Spitfire's eight ammo tanks, cock all the guns and replace all the panels in around three minutes flat.

'While we carried out our activities, the Flight Mech's Airframe were re-spraying the Spitfires with war camouflage and changing the squadron identity letters from WZ to QV. While the Flight Mech's Engine were helping Rolls-Royce personnel to change the two-bladed Watt's propeller to three-bladed de Havilland variable-pitch propellers, plus other modifications, we were removing the camera guns from the starboard wing stub and installing cine cameras inside the port wing stub. Some of the Spitfires were also still fitted with ring and bead sights, which had to be replaced with reflector sights.

'Our squadron was now flying to RAF Watton in Norfolk on a flight basis, changing daily with 66 Squadron and doing North Sea patrols, guarding shipping. We dispersed the planes every day to the boundary of Duxford airfield, bringing them back into the hangars every night.' New Browning guns for 19 and 66 Squadrons were then collected from the BSA Factory at Small Heath, Birmingham. 'These guns had no flash eliminator, but a new type of muzzle choke which gave them a faster rate of fire and made for less fouling in the choke than in the old flash eliminator. It made maintenance easier and gave longer life to the barrel. It also meant that the gun ports could now be covered, whereas before the flash eliminators of the two outer guns, port and starboard side, protruded forward of the leading edges of the wings. These guns meant a lot of hard work for us all in the squadron armoury. For the next few weeks there was the stripping and thorough cleaning of the guns to be done. The feeds had to be altered on a lot of the guns as 50 per cent had to be left-hand feed and 50 per cent right-hand feed. Then the old guns had to be removed from the Spitfires and the new guns installed, the aircraft taken to the firing butts and their new guns harmonized with the reflector sight, and the installation and harmonization then checked by the pilot. The eight guns were then lock-nutted, wired, then test-fired. I spent days on my knees under the wings doing this work. We'd push the Spitfires to the butts and manually lift them onto the trestles for leveling before harmonizing – all hard work.'

Fred and other ground crew worked round the clock to finish the gun changing and harmonizing because the aircraft was required the next morning. 'Part of our hangar was then being used in the evening by the WAAFs being taught drill procedures. Of course, there was the occasional wolf whistle from some of the lads while the girls were marching away from the Sergeant WAAF in charge, but we'd get a right earful the times she heard us. She was a right battleaxe. Her language could be stronger than ours!'

Early in December 1939, Fred received his first promotion to AC/1 armourer. After Christmas, freezing cold weather and snow set in. Flying was impossible for days.

'One day early February, I saw this new pilot, a flying officer, in front of me walking with a very queer lurching gait. It was Flying Officer Douglas Bader, who had lost both legs in a flying accident in December 1931 – he now walked on two metal legs. We were wondering what position he would hold on the squadron, not realizing he intended to fly. Later that day he gave us a magnificent display of aerobatics in the Squadron Miles Magister.

'Later in February 1940, I was detailed to go to Whittlesford, where Spitfire K9809 had dived into the ground the previous night while practicing take-offs and landings. The pilot, Pilot Officer Trenchard, was killed. I was horrified. The plane was in small pieces, the engine everywhere: one belt of ammo was wrapped around an oleo leg [a telescopic shock absorber used on landing gear], the wheel of which was four-hundred yards away.'

On 25 May 1940, 19 Squadron moved to Hornchurch in order to provide air cover with other squadrons for the evacuation at Dunkirk. 'The next morning it was 0500 hours at Dispersal and Daily Inspections in the dark, which would be our norm for the next couple of weeks. It was very early when the squadron took off that first morning but Flight Sergeant George Unwin, whose Spitfire I worked on, was unlucky. There were fourteen pilots but only twelve Spitfires and he lost the draw for places. I can't remember who flew QV-H in his place but on returning I could see that all the guns had been fired (because the patches covering the gun ports had all been blown away). It was a quick re-arm, but as the planes returned, mostly individually, it was a case of all mucking in on a single aircraft – a quick clean out of the gun barrels, a drop of oil on the breech block and once again, ready.

*Top left:* Spitfire pilots pose beside the wreckage of a Junkers Ju 87 Stuka, which they shot down near Manston Airfield, 5 February 1941.

*Top right:* The top-scoring Allied ace of the Second World War, Wing Commander Johnnie Johnson, seen here with his pet Labrador, Sally.

*Centre left:* Spitfire Mark XII, MB882, the plane Terry Spencer flew when he shot down Luftwaffe ace Emil Lang.

*Bottom left:* Pilots of No. 19 Squadron 'scramble' for the photographer, from the back of a lorry at Fowlmere, Cambridgeshire.

*Above:* Mary Ellis, one of the last surviving pilots of the ATA, celebrating her 100th birthday with Boultbee's Matt Jones after their flight.

*Below:* Former Spitfire pilot Ray Roberts taking part in the centenary celebrations at Biggin Hill in his 100th year.

*Above:* Mary Ellis, reunited with her Spitfire, was handed the controls of the two-seater aircraft during her flight with Matt Jones.

*Below:* ATA pilots Joy Lofthouse (née Gough), Mary Ellis and Molly Rose reunited at Goodwood in August 2015.

*Left:* Pilots of No. 303 Polish Fighter Squadron gathering around the inscribed tail-fin of their 178th victim, a Junkers Ju 88, at RAF Kirton-in-Lindsey, 26 August 1942.

*Below:* Spitfire PR Mark XI, EN654, being flown by Jeffrey Quill, Vickers-Supermarine's Chief Test Pilot, on a test flight.

*Below left*: Pilots of No. 19 Squadron (Frank Brinsden holds Springer Spaniel Rangy, Sub-Lieutenant A. G. Blake, aka the 'Admiral', seated centre). Dogs played a vital role in boosting morale amongst RAF squadrons in the war.

*Below right*: One in a series of official photos taken in December 1942, intended to illustrate the vital but unsung daily activities of a typical 'erk' (ground crew).

*Above:* Terry Spencer and his wife Lesley, taken shortly after they were married in 1947.

*Right*: Terry in his Spitfire XIV, the day before it was shot down at Wismar Bay.

*Below*: Ground staff re-arm a Spitfire Mk I at Biggin Hill, September 1940.

*Right:* Armourer Fred Roberts re-arms Supermarine Spitfire Mark IA, X4474 'QV-I', of No. 19 Squadron at Fowlmere, Cambridgeshire.

*Below:* Armourers set the tail fuses on a clutch of 500-pounders in front of a Spitfire XVI of No. 603 Squadron at Ludham, March 1945.

*Below left:* Flight-Lieutenant J. C. Dundas, fighter pilot, who flew with No. 609 Squadron from 1939-40.

*Below centre:* Squadron Leader H. S. L. 'Cocky' Dundas, Commanding Officer of No. 56 Squadron, at Duxford, Cambridgeshire.

*Below right:* ATA pilot Monique Agazarian.

*Above:* Joy Lofthouse takes to the skies seventy years after her last Spitfire flight.

*Below*: The Grace Spitfire, with pilot Carolyn Grace at the controls, at Farnborough, 2006.

*Above:* Sergeant Alan Robinson shakes hands with Boultbee's Matt Jones after their flight.

*Below:* Alan becomes the first in the Spitfire Scholarship to fly solo.

'I believe every one of our aircraft that returned that day had bullet or cannon shell holes in them somewhere. Some of them were a mass of patches by the time the riggers had finished with them. At the end of that first day, we had three pilots missing, two pilots wounded and five Spitfires destroyed against the claim of ten enemy planes destroyed. That day also saw us receive the first of a new breed of Spitfires with hydraulic operated undercarriage superseding the manual operated pump to lower and raise the undercarriage.

'Those long days were very tiring, even if much of the time we were only waiting for the Spitfires to take off or return. It was sunny and hot most of the time. It was strange, knowing that the Spitfires were actually going into action. "Who will return?" was always on your mind.'

On 24 June, the squadron moved to Fowlmere, a satellite station to Duxford. Living conditions were rough and primitive. Fortunately, the weather was kind, which helped. Later on, Fred learned that Fowlmere could be cruel on cold, wet and windy days. By July, however, the squadron moved back to Duxford. The Battle of Britain was about to start: the Luftwaffe would begin their frequent daylight attacks on the airfields.

Nineteen Squadron had started receiving a new experimental Mk IB series of Spitfires in late June. These were fitted with two 20 mm Hispano cannon, with much more destructive power than the machine guns in the eight-gun Spitfires. The experiment would create problems for the ground teams and the pilots. 'None of our armourers on the squadron had any knowledge of these cannon. On

9 July, I lost my pride and joy, Spitfire K9853 QV-H. While taxiing out for take-off, Pilot Officer Howard Williams, in K9799, taxied into Flight Sergeant Unwin, in K9853, and demolished the tail and rear end of the fuselage; both Spitfires were write-offs. I was now to have one of the new cannon Spitfires to maintain. Not having any knowledge of the Hispano cannon or its working or any printed information to guide us didn't make maintenance too easy and we discovered the cannons weren't working properly in the Spitfires; the pilots were having a lot of stoppages during air firing practice.'

Being sent on a one week 20 mm cannon course at RAF Manby wasn't much help. 'Other than being given names to all the parts of the cannon, we knew more about the gun than the instructors did! By the time we returned from Manby, there had been no further success in reducing the stoppages on the cannons by our fellow armourers.

'We still had some eight-gun Spitfires on the squadron which was fortunate because the cannon stoppages seemed to be unsolvable. We took a lot of stick from the pilots over these stoppages. For a while, they wanted to blame the armourers for the trouble and then, when a full magazine of 20 mm ammunition was expended, the pilots complained they only had six seconds of firing time against the eighteen seconds with the old Browning guns. We had little help or encouragement from our armament staff at Duxford. Even the experts who came from RAF Northolt to help us could only listen and learn.

'The 31st August dawned bright and clear, a beautiful sunny morning. At about 0800 hours our squadron was scrambled to cover RAF Debden, where they met a force of Luftwaffe fighters and bombers. Due to cannon stoppages, we lost three Spitfires, Flying Officer Coward being severely wounded and bailing out, Flying Officer Brinsden taking to his parachute but landing unhurt, and Pilot Officer Aerberhardt, whilst attempting to land at Fowlmere without flaps, crashed and was burned to death. This we all witnessed – but could do nothing to help.'

One week later, 19 Squadron was being called on much more often as the Germans changed their tactics, beginning heavy and frequent raids on London and the south-east towns, instead of the airfields. 'We ground staff regularly gathered around any spare aircraft after our planes had taken off and listened to the dialogue between pilots and pilots, pilots and control, while our aircraft engaged with the enemy. This was conveyed to us by one of the Wireless Operators from the Signal Section who was listening on the spare aircraft radio. This also gave us an indication of the time of return of the aircraft and, in some cases, the state of the aircraft and pilot.

'There was more action on 3rd September and 5th September but sadly on the fifth we lost our Commanding Officer, Squadron Leader Pinkham, who was shot down over Kent. He bailed out, severely wounded, but was too low for his parachute to open properly and he was later found dead.' Pinkham had joined the RAF on a short service commission in 1935. On 3 June 1940, he was given command of 19 Squadron, Duxford. He had already been awarded the AFC (Air Force Cross) a month later.

He was twenty-five when his plane was shot down. 'Flight

Lieutenant Lane was promoted that day to the rank of Squadron Leader and assumed command of the squadron.'

All Mark IB cannon-armed Spitfires were withdrawn the following day. 'It was ironic that this should happen just one day after Squadron Leader Pinkham was killed when, for so long, he had pleaded for the withdrawal of the Mark IB Spitfires because of their unreliable armament. We had these Mark IB aircraft replaced by a lot of old Mark IA Spitfires that were flown from an Operational Training Unit at RAF Hawarden by pilots of the Air Transport Auxiliary, some of them lady pilots.

'The OTU personnel must have selected their worst aircraft to send. I know the aircraft flew, but only just, and the armament was in a terrible state, badly maintained. They had rusty gun barrels, fouled up muzzle chokes, lack of oiling. We even found ammunition tanks so badly buckled that the ammunition belts wouldn't have run smoothly and would have caused stoppages. Other trades found faults equally as glaring. The planes certainly had not had the high standard of maintenance that everyone gave on 19 Squadron.'

A week or so later, Fred was maintaining a brand new Mark IA eight-gun Spitfire when a scramble took place (a rapid deployment of fighter planes to counter an offensive raid). 'The engine cowlings were off, the gun fairings were off, the guns were unloaded and the ammo tanks removed. The Flight Mech's Engine and Airframe and myself were all at work when Flight Sergeant Unwin came running, yelling for his plane. I'm sure we must have broken a record for bringing a Spit to serviceability. George was airborne in less than ten minutes with a straight take-off across the wind and no engine warm-up. I don't know if he caught up with the squadron or took on the Luftwaffe on his own, but it showed the courage of the man and the confidence he placed in us, his ground crew. Later we heard that Flight Sergeant Unwin had been awarded the Distinguished Flying Medal. Up to then he'd shot down twelve enemy aircraft. We were really proud.'

Later that month, the new Mark II Spitfires arrived at Duxford to replace the Mark Is. 'These were fitted with a more powerful Rolls-Royce engine and Koffman Cartridge Starters. No more lugging around those heavy accumulator trolleys from aircraft to aircraft at scrambles.' Then in early October, a Spitfire armed with two cannons and four Browning guns and a new belt feed mechanism was delivered to Duxford.

As the Battle of Britain drew to a close, Fred Roberts' time with 19 Squadron abruptly ended. In October 1940, he was posted on detachment to 151 Squadron at RAF North Weald. From there he was briefly posted to Wales, then Stratford-upon-Avon, training new recruits, and in August 1942, days after his marriage to his sweetheart, Mary, Fred was posted overseas to India, an NCO in charge of a team of armourers. He left the RAF in March 1946. Yet it would always be his time with 19 Squadron, arming Spitfires in the Battle of Britain, that he would recall time and again. 'I'm always proud that I was in the Battle of Britain,' he said in 2003. 'Always proud.'

## Who Stole My Trousers?

John Milne was nineteen when he arrived at RAF Duxford Aerodrome in March 1940 from Halton, where he had recently completed his training as an RAF Flight Rigger, LAC. He was posted to 19 Squadron at Duxford, the first unit to be equipped with Supermarine Spitfires in August 1938. At Duxford he became the rigger for the Spitfire of the Commanding Officer, Squadron Leader Brian 'Sandy' Lane.

'I arrived at Duxford via Whittlesford Station. My parents lived at Cambridge, so there could not have been a better introduction to the active RAF than 19 Squadron. I slept at first on a "let down": a metal bed in a crew room off the hangar. Then I transferred to a ground floor room – a barrack-block (not occupied by 19 Squadron) where I awoke one morning to find my trousers gone!

'Most of us had only one uniform. I waited until all those awake had left the room then stole another man's trousers. I wonder how the episode finished? Soon I transferred to a 19 Squadron room on the first floor of another block and things were much better. We kept the room immaculately clean and tidy – the men were all regular airmen and well practised in the domestic side of service life. I was introduced to snooker, played upstairs above the NAAFI (canteen) and a most popular pastime. Every morning we marched off to the hangar under the senior airman present and pulled the Spitfires from the hangar. And every night we moved them back in again. Soon they were moved permanently to a dispersal area around the southwest of the airfield and we had a prefabricated hut to use as crewmen by day and by night.

'Squadron Leader Stephenson was our Commanding Officer and Flight Lieutenant Lane commanded "A" flight to which I was allocated. Douglas Bader joined "A" Flight and used to arrive at the dispersal area in his black MG.

'The war seemed at first to be remote and we routinely carried out daily and periodic inspections of the aircraft and performed all the incidental duties involved in servicing the aircraft and attending their take-offs and landings. An exhilarating duty was lying across the tailplane, breathless, while the pilot ran the engine at high revs.

'The Spitfire airframe and its installations and equipment, so far as they came under the care of a flight rigger, were not difficult to repair and maintain. The Merlin engine, with its accessories, was, I think, a bit more temperamental, particularly as regards oil and coolant leaks and loss of revs. A crew of rigger and mechanic looked after each aircraft, or sometimes two. Various specialist tradesmen – electricians, wireless mechanics, instrument repairers and armourers – would appear, fiddle with their allotted bits and pieces, then disappear. Wireless testing on the ground would go thus: "Hello Dory, Hello Dory, five three calling and testing, are you receiving me, are you receiving me, over." "Hello five three, hello five three, am receiving you loud and clear, strength nine, over and out."

'The armourer's job could be arduous. Ammunition is heavy, and loading the guns with them and their ammunition tightly packed in the thin wings was hard on the hands. When the guns had been fired, the riggers pasted squares of aircraft linen over the holes, giving a row of four square red patches at the leading edge of each wing.

'These patches maintained the smooth shape of the wing leading edge, essential to peak performance, and also prevented the guns from becoming colder and jamming through freezing.

'Starting the engine on an early Spitfire involved using a Trolley-Ac, a two-wheeled enclosed low hand-cart containing accumulators. One starter trolley was shared between several aircraft, so the crews became adept at high-speed trolley-pulling from one Spitfire to the next. Later Spitfires had Koffman cartridge starters, thus eliminating the Trolley-Ac performance. The Trolley-Ac had a thick cable that plugged in through a flap in the engine-cowling. Once the engine had started, one of the crew pulled the cable out and took it away, being careful not to step back into the propeller! After starting the engine, the pilot would signal the ground crew to lie on the tailplane while he ran the engine at high speed. This really took one's breath away. After "chocks away", the two crew would take the wingtips and see the aircraft away from its parking area, until waved away by the pilot. Wheel chocks were originally individual items, with a man each to pull a rope which was so wrapped around the chock as to swivel it away from under the wheel and prevent it from jamming. The later system was to have both chocks connected by a steel angle iron, which enabled the pair of ground crew to execute a co-ordinated and speeded-up chock removal action.

'A feature of the Spitfire design was the narrow wheel-track, dictated by the wing design. This did not make for stability in a rough landing, but the pilots just had to put up with it. The Me 109 had a similarly narrow wheel-track. Many Spitfires required wingtip repairs after tipping over in bumpy landings.

'An arduous job was pumping up the oleo legs – the undercarriage. It was not the pumping that was hard, but dragging the heavy equipment around the airfield. It consisted of a long vertical pump arm, a pump and a pressure-gauge to check the air pressure in the leg, all mounted on a large and heavy plank of wood, just like a railway sleeper.

'One needed a strong back to service the Spitfire. The daily inspection included lifting the tail with one's back under the tailplane, to check the tail wheel's functioning, and also similarly lifting each main plane in turn, beside the undercarriage attachment, to check the pintle bolt [holding the leg to the wing-spar] by its creaking or silence when dropped again. Some jobs were more complicated: one I remember was changing a stern-frame [the whole tail] in the hangar at Duxford.

'Duxford life became busier, with two Spitfire squadrons and 264 Defiant Squadron. Nineteen Squadron moved to Fowlmere, back to Duxford, and eventually settled at Fowlmere. When we first moved to Fowlmere, there was no permanent accommodation. We slept in bell tents, feet to the central pole. A mobile cookhouse accompanied us – one day it caught fire! We dug latrine trenches and spent most of our time out of doors. Nobody seemed to mind. Fowlmere later had Nissen huts, never popular, as condensation dripped down from the underside of the cold steel roof onto one's bedding and oneself.

'Flying from Fowlmere must have been fun! The airfield was far from level, and dipped down considerably in the corner nearest to Duxford. Part of it was laid with metal mesh decking to improve the surface. There were certain features of Duxford and Fowlmere which must remain forever recallable by everyone: the sound of Merlin engines starting, taxiing and flying low over the airfield; the smell of glycol coolant leaking onto hot metal; the smell of 100 octane petrol, and the staining from its green dye.

'On 29 July 1940, I bought a motorcycle from King and Harper in Cambridge. It was a Royal Enfield 350cc trials model, with knobbly tyres and a steel plate under the sump. I rode it home from the garage to show my parents and then to Duxford. I had hardly entered Duxford when I was told to paint over the shining aluminium mudguards with green camouflage paint!

'Nineteen Squadron operated for a time from Horsham St Faith on the outskirts of Norwich, which was under construction as a permanent RAF Station. There were no hangars, workshops or living accommodation available so the crews stayed for short tours in a hutted camp at Old Catton, Norwich, whence we travelled to and from Horsham St Faith by lorry. Whilst there I saw my first Cierva Autogyro [an autogyro looks like a rudimentary helicopter but its rotors are not powered. Instead, the thrust comes from a propellor either at the front or rear].

'During one tour at Fowlmere, "B" flight moved to Eastchurch for a short while. The ground crew and equipment were transported in a couple of splendid aircraft. Ground crew to whom I can put a name were: Flight Sergeant Dennard, in charge of "A" flight personnel, and known as "Nodder" from his involuntary habit. He was a most able and experienced NCO and kept us all in order. Corporal Rich was our immediate superior, again an able and experienced NCO. My daily companions included C.D. "Dickie" Bird, from Witham, Essex; George Henderson, from Reigate, Surrey, with an Aerial square-four motorcycle; Puttick, with a Norton motorcycle; J. "Sandy" Sanderson, from Lockwood, Huddersfield, and G. S. "Screwdriver" Tynan-Blunden, also known as "Senora".

'Odd memories remain: "digging for victory" – our vegetable patch near the dispersal hut; WAAFs playing hockey on the airfield; hot suppers from a huge Thermos flask in the dispersal hut, and frequent visits to the Chequers and the Black Horse in Fowlmere. Altogether, those few months were one of the best times of my life and so very different from anything that had gone before.'

After the war, John Milne went to university at Cambridge and trained as an architect. He died, aged ninety-one, in August 2012.

# CHAPTER 5

⊙

# Spitfire Families

THE SECOND WORLD WAR DOMINATED AND irrevocably changed the lives of so many families across the country. The story of the Spitfire and its success is also often one involving one or more members of the same family, with some extraordinary stories of sibling pilots and test pilots serving together through the Battle of Britain, up until the last days of the war. Despite heart-breaking loss, these stories of the brothers and sisters on the frontline show their determination to play a part in winning the war for Britain.

## The Dundas Brothers

John Dundas, DFC and Bar (born 1915) and his younger brother Sir Hugh, CBE, DSO and Bar, DFC (born 1920) grew up in North Yorkshire. John initially worked as a journalist for the *Yorkshire Post* for two years before joining the RAF Auxiliary Air Force, 609 Squadron, in 1938. Called into full-time service in August 1939, he proved to be an exceptionally skilled pilot at Dunkirk and in the Battle of Britain. In October 1940, he was awarded the DFC.

On 28 November 1940, while flying a Spitfire, he downed an Me 109 off the coast of the Isle of Wight. It was his final victory. Minutes later, he was shot down into the sea by German fighters, who also claimed the life of John Dundas' wingman, Pilot Officer Baillon. Dundas' body was never recovered.

John's younger brother, Hugh, or 'Cocky' as he was known (the nickname was derived from his resemblance to a rooster, not as a description of an arrogant or conceited man), had hoped to be a solicitor, but decided to join his older brother in the fight against Hitler. At twenty he joined 616 (South Yorkshire) RAF Auxiliary Squadron to fight in the Battle of Britain and scored a number of victories. However, in mid-August 1940 he was shot down and wounded, and his injuries kept him out of the final phase of the battle. He later took part in offensive fighter sweeps over France as Flight Commander of 616 Squadron and thereafter as a Squadron Commander and Wing Leader at Duxford. In 1943, he was posted to North Africa, to command a wing of five Spitfire squadrons, and then posted to Malta and Italy. He is credited with having shot down at least six enemy aircraft from 1940 to 1943. By November 1944, aged twenty-four, he was the youngest group captain to have ever served in the RAF.

In 1941, Hugh's 616 Squadron was part of the RAF Tangmere Wing, commanded by Wing Commander Douglas Bader. During the summer of that year, Hugh frequently flew with Bader's section. Many years later he recalled what he had learned from one of the world's most famous Spitfire pilots and what he personally believed was required to be a good fighter pilot. 'Through him I learned the importance of teamwork, mutual support. Although he was tremendously aggressive, he was also very skilled and determined and then, right up to the moment of engagement, more or less directing who was going to do what. You can't be a successful fighter pilot unless you are a very good shot. You've got to get stuck in, no holding back really. But as well as being aggressive you had to be careful – a paradox in itself. You've got to be streetwise while being aggressive. You also had to try to survive – and you got wise about how to do that. You had to have quick reactions, too. It was a whole collection of qualities.

'The Spitfire was a lovely plane to fly. The only thing was, at that early stage we still had canvas or fabric ailerons. It wasn't until the beginning of 1941 that we got metal ailerons, which made a tremendous difference to the handling of the Spit at high speed in a dive. With canvas it became heavy laterally. It had other shortcomings. When we went to Dunkirk we didn't have self-sealing petrol tanks, we didn't have rear view mirrors. One of the first things we did after one or two engagements at Dunkirk was to go down to the local motor agency and get rear view mirrors and have them screwed to the top of the windscreen. But it was a very robust aeroplane – it could accommodate a great deal of punishment. Geoff Quill once told me that the last mark of the Spitfire – all out weight – was equivalent of a Mark I with twenty-one extra people with their luggage. But basically the same plane.'

After the war, he went into a career in newspaper publishing, later moving into commercial television as a successful executive before becoming director of Thames Television. He died in July 1995.

## The Gough Girls

Joy and Yvonne Gough were two young sisters from Cirencester, Gloucestershire, born fifteen months apart, who had never even driven a car, let alone been near a plane before. In their wildest dreams, they'd never imagined they'd get the chance to pilot a Spitfire. But that's exactly what happened to the sport-mad Gough Girls, as they were known locally. For by the latter part of the Second World War, Joy and Yvonne were working as ferry pilots for the Air Transport Auxiliary, delivering Spitfires and other planes around the country, the only sisters to fly for the ATA.

Their wartime path to the ATA didn't start until the autumn of 1943. Joy, who was twenty, had been working in the local Lloyds Bank since the war begun. Older sister Yvonne had been married for just a year to a young RAF bomber pilot, Tom Wheatley. Tragically, Tom was killed in a bombing raid over Berlin in March 1943. Yet Yvonne refused to let grief overwhelm her and became determined to do something for the war effort.

She was living with Tom's mother in Kent that summer. While working in a local munitions factory, freezing and testing batteries, she spotted a life-changing advertisement in *Aeroplane* magazine. 'It was the same advertisement that Joy saw, though neither of us knew we'd both applied at the time. The ad said that the Air Transport Auxiliary wanted more ferry pilots and that they were willing to train people *ab initio* – that meant from the beginning. In other words, without any flying experience.'

Over 2,000 people wrote off in response to the advertisement. The Gough sisters were amongst the seventeen people who were accepted. 'Tom's mother said I joined up to fly because I thought I'd be killed, too,' said Yvonne. 'But this wasn't about a death wish. I saw it as one of the most worthwhile jobs I could possibly have. It seemed natural to me to do my bit for the war by flying.'

Because Yvonne had applied under her married name from a different address, no one in the ATA connected the two as sisters. Joy, for her part, was drawn to aviation because in Cirencester, surrounded by airfields, she'd already met so many young male flyers. 'I wanted to keep up, know more about what the boys in uniform talked about. That's why I started reading *Aeroplane*. You couldn't just stand there, useless, dumb, when the boys were talking about planes.

'The ad said you had to be over five feet six inches, educated to at least "O" Level and be willing to undergo a strict medical. They were particularly interested in people with a good sporting background: people with really good sporting skills.'

Yvonne's application went in a few weeks before Joy's. Because Joy still lived at home in Cirencester and Yvonne in Kent, it came as a bit of a surprise when they both realized what had happened. 'There I was, coming out of the station at the White Waltham HQ one day, having started my training, and there was Joy, coming in for her initial interview!' recalled Yvonne.

After training, the sisters were assigned to different women-only ferry pools: Joy to Hamble in the south, Yvonne to Cosford, near Wolverhampton. 'It turned out to be a nice summer that May, 1944,' said Joy. 'You'd walk into the operations room, the hatch would open and the ops officer would hand out the chits for what you'd be delivering. Each day varied. Sometimes we were taken to the factory at Eastleigh to collect a Spitfire. We'd also transport the planes to the maintenance unit where the radio and guns were fitted, but we weren't trained to use those things. It would have involved much longer training to train us for radio.

'I did have my scary times. One day I was given a chit to pick up a new Spitfire from the factory and I found myself in a fix right after take-off: I was heading towards some barrage balloons. The later versions of the Spitfire, the Marks XII to XIV, had much more powerful engines. "This is a different beast altogether, Joy," they warned me. "Open up the throttle gently because it will have a pronounced swing on take-off. And you have to use the opposite rudder to straighten it out."'

Joy did everything she had been taught: opposite rudder to counteract the swing. 'But to my horror, the Spit was still heading towards the barrage balloons. It felt like minutes of sheer terror. In fact, it was a matter of seconds. Because the minute the plane gets height, the controls come into play – and the controls keep it straight. So in reality, you straighten up quite quickly. But for that minute or two, my brain was racing; "Am I going to hit that cable? Or whizz through it?" But you're so busy doing what you think is the right thing, you don't actually panic. That was where the training came into play. You'd been trained to deal with it.'

As Third Officers, the sisters earned £9 a week (in 1943, the ATA women pilots were awarded equal pay with the pay of the men, the first ever instance of equal pay for women in the UK). They'd ferry planes for twelve or thirteen days at a stretch, then have a few days' leave.

By then, Joy was engaged to George (Jiri Hartman), a Czech Spitfire pilot with 310 Squadron. Flying had more or less taken over her life. In the run up to D-Day in the summer of 1944, the pace for the ferry pilots got even more hectic. 'We'd been delivering planes that spring upwards of twenty fighters a day; Typhoons, Tempests and Spitfires flown straight to the squadrons on the south coast airfields,' Joy explained.

Yet when the war finally ended, both girls had mixed feelings. Both had loved their job. 'I was sad that it was all over. The last plane I ever flew was a Spitfire, from Scotland down to Yorkshire. Everything was closing down by then. It really was like resigning from a job you loved,' recalled Yvonne.

When Hamble shut down, Joy found herself briefly ferrying Barracudas and Seafires (adapted to land on aircraft carriers) up to Scotland. 'There were fields upon fields in Scotland with aircraft with their wings folded up – eventually destroyed and used for scrap. For me, the end of flying for the ATA was devastating. The excitement of this amazing wartime job had gone.'

The sisters married and started families soon after war ended. Yvonne married Neil McDonald, a pilot from the Royal Canadian Air Force and moved to Canada. Joy married George in Prague, Czechoslovakia, and remained there with their small son briefly – until the Czech Communist government, backed by the Soviets, took over and it was obvious it was wise to return to England for good.

For the rest of their lives, the Gough girls would reminisce together about the ATA days and the time when they flew Spitfires. 'People often say, does it seem real now, flying Spitfires while war and chaos was all around you?' said Joy. 'I always say yes, they were such impressionable years, they can never quite leave you'.

'Flying the Spitfire was a kind of freedom you never get any other way,' said Yvonne. 'More than anything, with the Spit, it was always as if you had wings sewn on your back. That was exactly how it felt. It was so manoeuvrable. Once, on a cloudy, rainy day, I ran my right wing through a rain cloud: rain on the right wing, on the left there was sunshine. You could do almost anything with those planes. Sometimes, when you were landing the Spitfire at dusk – we were supposed to land twenty minutes before dusk – you felt it was almost as if you could play with the whole world, an otherworldly feeling.' Both sisters flew over fifty Spitfires as ferry pilots, which as Joy modestly pointed out, 'was nothing compared to the other girls who flew'.

## The Agazarian Family

Growing up in Surrey in the 1920s, the Agazarian children would enjoy games outside with their favourite toy, a First World War Sopwith Pup fighter plane, which their French-born mother had bought at an auction for £5 and installed at the bottom of their garden. The family were both cosmopolitan and prosperous: the children's Armenian father, Berge, ran a successful engineering company and the youthful Agazarian obsession with aviation would be one that would eventually shape all their lives.

Born in 1920, Monique, the youngest, was educated at the Convent of the Sacred Heart in Roehampton, London, and at a Paris finishing school. When war broke out, Monique's three brothers, Levon, Jack and Noel all signed up for the RAF Voluntary Reserve and their little sister vowed that somehow, she too would fly.

At first, Monique nursed with the Voluntary Aid Detachment (VAD) at Uxbridge and upon learning that the Air Transport Auxiliary were recruiting women, she applied to join. She was turned down. She was below the minimum height requirement and at that point she had no flying experience at all. Yet she persisted, and when the shortage of ATA ferry pilots hit its peak in 1943 and they became willing to train pilots without experience, Monique got in. She started flying with the ATA in October 1943.

By that time, Monique's older brother, Levon, was a fighter pilot, flying Thunderbolt fighters in Calcutta and Burma. Brother Jack had been seconded from the RAF to join the covert Special Operations Executive as a clandestine wireless operator in France. But the war was to take a terrible toll on the Agazarian family. In July 1943, Jack was captured and tortured by the Germans, refusing to reveal any information. He was imprisoned for eighteen months, only to be executed just days before the war ended.

Noel had joined 609 Squadron as a fighter pilot. He had a distinguished career flying Spitfires and shooting down seven aircraft in the Battle of Britain (his Spitfire from 1940 is currently on display at the Imperial War Museum in London). Then he volunteered for a posting in the Middle East in January 1941, joining 274 Squadron in the Western Desert. On 6 May, Noel was shot down and killed when his squadron was intercepted in Gambut. He is buried in the Knightsbridge War Cemetery, Acoma, Libya.

Yet like so many others whose families faced the worst, Monique Agazarian did not let personal loss or fear hinder her determination to play her part in the ATA. For nearly two years she ferried Spitfires, Hurricanes, Seafires, Typhoons and Mustangs for the ATA until September 1945. Then, still fiercely determined to continue flying, she obtained her commercial pilot's licenses, and became one of a very small number of ATA female flyers to forge a career in aviation after the war.

In June 1945, Monique joined Island Air Services, set up to run pleasure flights over London, out of Heathrow and Croydon airports, as well as charter flights. IAS also flew flowers from the Scilly Isles to the mainland. In due course she became the owner and managing director of the company before closing it in the late fifties. After several years as a commercial pilot, she joined Air Training Services, a company set up to provide flight training in ground simulators, the first of which was set up in the Grosvenor Hotel in London. In 1976, she took over ATS and ran various other ground training centres until selling the business in 1992. She died in London in 1993, aged seventy-two.

In 2008, there was a formal acknowledgement of the ATA women's work flying Spitfires during the Second World War when then Prime Minister Gordon Brown awarded each surviving female Spitfire pilot with a medal at Downing Street.

Since then, there been many books, documentaries and literary works dedicated to the courage of the Spitfire women. Alison Hill's poetry collection, *Sisters in Spitfires*, celebrate many of these ATA women. These are her poems about the Gough Girls and Monique Agazarian.

### Sisters in Spitfires

*The only sisters to fly with ATA, Joy and Yvonne*
*were posted to different pools under different names*
*but shared an enduring love of the Spitfire.*

*A plane that turned many into poets and dreamers,*
*they flew with wings sewn on their backs, felt snug in*
*the cockpit, handling their Spits with care.*

*Joy jumped at the chance to join the ATA,*
*glad to be at Hamble in 1944, glad to learn to fly*
ab initio *before she could drive a car.*

*Older sister Yvonne, posted to less-than-glamorous*
*Cosford, flew in thick Midlands fog, but at least*
*they were both airborne, making it through the war.*

## Model Pilot, Model Lawn

*The Sacred Heart sisters found her a delightful*
*child but very pleasure-loving. Peter Pan inspired*
*dreams of flying, lent her silver-tipped wings.*

*Her passion for planes began in the back garden,*
*in an old Sopwith Pup her mother found at auction;*
*Monique and her brothers happily flew the world.*

*From volunteer nurse to ferry pilot, Monique stood*
*taller for the ATA, borrowing an inch or three*
*for her medical, flying Spitfires with ease.*

*She ferried cigarettes once or twice too, stashed*
*in an overnight bag or down by her parachute,*
*a welcome favour for those waiting to fly.*

*Long after the war she manicured her window box*
*with nail scissors; a friend's flight of fancy adding*
*a miniature blue Spitfire set into the grass.*

*She'd flown all types of front-liners in the war,*
*yet did not take a coach trip until May 1991.*
*Why be driven when you can fly?*

*Monique wanted the sound of a Merlin engine*
*at her funeral – arriving, passing, fading –*
*lingering essence of her energy, her vibrant life.*

## The Grace Family

For Spitfire lovers, the Grace Spitfire is widely acknowledged as one of the best-known examples of a restored Second World War Spitfire regularly taking to the skies. Yet the story behind its success is one of a family determined to uphold the legacy of the man who originally restored it – a legacy achieved against the odds.

Even in the twenty-first century, a female pilot operating a two-seater Spitfire at airshows and flying displays remains something of a rarity, let alone her dedication – for much of her life – to keeping the fighter plane in the air. But Carolyn Grace, Spitfire pilot and head of the family organization which owns and operates the Grace Spitfire, has always insisted that the wonderful thing about flying a restored Spitfire has little to do with gender. It is all about the Spitfire's historic link with both past and present.

'Right from the start, when it was first restored, it has been so rewarding to get the veterans who had flown it involved. Because we're a two-seater Spit and can offer flights to people, we have flown many Second World War veterans who flew and maintained the Spitfire in anger in wartime. Our words are: "We honour the past that has enabled our future."' When you consider the history of the Grace Spitfire ML407, these words make perfect sense.

Built at the Castle Bromwich factory in early 1944 as a Mark IX single-seat fighter, it served in the front line of battle through the last twelve months of the war, flying with six different squadrons of the RAF's 2nd Tactical Air Force. It flew 176 operational sorties in a total of 319 combat hours. In April 1944, it was delivered to 485 (New Zealand) Squadron by Jackie Moggridge, a female ferry pilot of the ATA. One of the elite group of female ATA pilots, Jackie would eventually fly the Grace Spitfire with Carolyn over half a century on.

In December 1944, ML407 was transferred to 341 Free French Squadron. It then moved through various allied squadrons – 308 (Polish) Squadron, 349 (Belgian) Squadron, 345 (Free French) Squadron, 332 (Norwegian) Squadron and back to 485 (New Zealand) Squadron at the end of the war. It remained in a maintenance unit until 1950 when it was one of twenty Spitfires converted by Vickers-Armstrongs to the two-seat configuration as an advanced trainer for the Irish Air Corps until 1960. Eventually, it was acquired by Sir William Roberts for his museum in Strathallan, Scotland.

In 1979, Carolyn and Nick Grace were a young couple with a passion for aviation. Carolyn, who grew up in rural Australia, obtained her pilot's licence in 1978 and Nick, a design engineer, had always wanted to fly a Spitfire. He bought ML407 from the Strathallan museum and then spent five years carefully restoring the plane to flying condition in its two-seat configuration. Nick designed what is now known as the 'Grace in line Canopy Conversion', removing the bulbous rear canopy to a more streamlined version in order to keep the original line of the Spitfire intact.

By April 1985, the restored Spitfire flew again, piloted by Nick with Carolyn in the rear cockpit, watched by their two children; Richard, just nine months, and Olivia, aged two.

From then on, ML407 was a regular feature at airshows in the UK and Europe with Nick piloting the Spitfire.

Then everything changed. Nick was tragically killed in a car accident in 1988. Carolyn, suddenly widowed with two small children, was confronted with a tough situation. Keeping the Spitfire in the air was a complex and financially daunting enterprise. Surely, it would be best to sell the restored Spitfire? There were, of course, plenty of offers. 'There was a lot of expectation that that was what I would do as a widow with no money,' said Carolyn. 'I had offers – sometimes almost demands to sell it – and recommendations that I should sell it. Usually men telling me what I should be doing. But it was never in my thoughts, even in the darkest times, that the Spitfire would go. It would be like selling one of your children. As a family, we've moved six times to accommodate our Spitfire, twice in Cornwall, then to Chichester, then Horsham, then Essex and finally up to Northampton. But the issue of selling it back then was non-negotiable.'

Carolyn then set about the immense task of learning to fly the Spitfire. She had a total of 150 hours' flying time, mostly on tail-draggers (aeroplanes with an undercarriage configuration, like the Spitfire, that have a tail wheel rather than a nose wheel) spread over a twelve-year period, until she converted to flying the Spitfire in 1990 (with four-and-a-half hours conversion with an instructor) before going solo. 'It was going from a Stampe [a tail-dragger biplane] which is 145 horsepower, to the Spitfire which is 1,900 horsepower.'

By then, the Spitfire had become known as the Grace

Spitfire, in tribute to and in the memory of Nick. Once she'd achieved her solo, Carolyn then obtained her authorization to display the Grace Spitfire at aviation events and over another two years, she added her aerobatic and formation display qualification.

This was always going to be a family affair. Keeping the Grace Spitfire flying is a serious financial challenge yet even as teenagers, both Grace children shared their parents' determination to display it to the world. Olivia Grace, then fourteen, suggested the Grace Spitfire Supporters Club in 1997 to help the ongoing fundraising for the large annual costs involved in supporting the Spitfire. At thirteen, Richard Grace was already involved in the maintenance of the plane.

Today, Richard is Chief Engineer at the helm of Air Leasing Limited at Northampton, the maintenance organization for the Grace Spitfire. 'Without the maintenance support of Air Leasing, the Grace Spitfire could not fly. This, coupled with Richard's exceptional flying skills shown in his dynamic evocative displays in the Grace Spitfire and numerous other aircraft, secures the future of the plane into the next generation,' Carolyn explains.

Today, the Grace Spitfire is frequently seen flying at airshows and wartime anniversaries. Especially evocative are the summertime Battle Proms concerts sited at some of England's most beautiful stately homes where Carolyn has meticulously choreographed the Spitfire's manoeuvres to classical music. Over the years, Carolyn has flown surviving women who flew the Spitfire in wartime, women like Jackie Moggridge or Mary Ellis. Are there any shared qualities as

Spitfire pilots? 'They demonstrated modest determination. Combined with a natural ability for flying.'

Today, anyone can have their very own Spitfire experience in ML407. This, for Carolyn, is also an immensely rewarding aspect of the enterprise. 'People come with their grandparents, grandchildren, parents, babies and *everyone* is excited. The older generation revered it for what it did: but the beauty, the sound and how it looks and performs in the air are something every generation can relate to.'

# CHAPTER 6

⊙

# Love and Loss

SPITFIRE PILOTS KNEW ALL TOO WELL that every time they flew in combat it could be their last flight, and while on the ground their need to live for the present and hold onto happiness at every opportunity was fierce. Similarly, the constant threat of air raids affected the lives of the aircraft men and women on the ground, and often drew them together as they struggled to cope with the uncertainty of war. While some of these relationships were short-lived, many endured through to the end of the war and beyond, the bonds made during this time proving impossible to forget.

## The Girl on the Platform

July 1943, Biggin Hill. Twenty-two-year-old Sergeant Joe Roddis, a newly promoted engine fitter, was at work up on the main wing of a Spitfire, filling it up with petrol. Cheerful and lively, young Joe was already a Spitfire ground staff veteran. He'd worked on Spits during the Battle of Britain with 234 Squadron. After 1941, he'd been posted to the then newly formed 485 Squadron, working alongside the Kiwis (New Zealanders) and servicing their Spits.

Joe loved his job, with all its attendant perils and uncertainties. He relished the warm camaraderie he and the other ground staff had established with the New Zealand pilots. He had a girlfriend, who was working as a land girl. And, of course, he loved 'his' Spitfires. So perhaps it was entirely fitting that Joe was perched on a Spit that day when his eye was drawn to a small group of WAAFs walking down the perimeter track towards dispersal.

Naturally, there were wolf whistles and howls from the ground crews as the women made their way towards them. Five airwomen and one corporal in charge, all working as MT (motor transport) drivers. The women, accustomed to all the attention, drew closer. Then one of them, easily the prettiest, started laughing. She'd spotted Joe, bare-chested and smiley up there on his Spit. 'I heard her say to one of the other girls: "Ooh, I'm having some of that." Of course, I should have had my uniform on, not just my trousers, but it was a warm day. I looked at her and thought: "Yes! She's a very nice looking lass."'

Corporal Betty Wood and Sgt Joe Roddis were instantly drawn to each other. There was no time for more than the briefest of exchanges but both knew, since Betty's group of WAAFs were briefly attached to the squadron, there'd be opportunities later on to socialize. 'The women were at dispersal at all times, night and day and there were no problems at all. They would sleep in the same dispersal hut as the men but there was never any hanky-panky. Everybody behaved themselves, no swearing within earshot of 'em, and they did an excellent job, driving, tractor towing 500 gallon fuel tankers for the Spitfires. Some of the lads would get together with them, going to dances when we were off duty,' recalled Joe.

That same evening Sgt Roddis walked up from the Sergeants' Mess and stood at the guardroom. 'Betty, I knew, had to book out. I waited. Then I heard her. There's a big difference between a woman's tread and a bloke clomping along. And there she was, gorgeous and smiling – she was always a happy girl, she'd light up a place wherever you were.'

Conversation with Betty flowed naturally, and soon they were chatting away as if they'd known each other for years. Just a year older than Joe, Betty told him she loved to go dancing. She'd been in a formation team at one stage, a semi-professional. 'Okay, we'll go to The Teapot, eh?' said Joe. He wasn't mad keen on dancing really.

He just wanted to be with Betty. 'When we had a dance, the WAAFs could go in civvies. Our dance hall was The Teapot, fifteen minutes' walk from the station at Biggin Hill. When we had the time off, we'd go to dances up in London. But The Teapot was our nearest and dearest.'

There was no doubt in Joe's mind that Betty had stolen his heart. Yet it was made clear, right from the start, that taking it beyond a dancing friendship would be out of the question. 'She made it known, that first dance at The Teapot. "Do you know what this is?" she asked me, pointing to the ring on her finger. "Of course," I said. "Well, no hanky panky. Or else!"

'Betty's fiancé Laurie was the same rank and trade as me. But he'd been posted overseas to North Africa, Alamein. They'd been together since schooldays. Yet Betty and me …

well, we seemed to be so good for each other.' Whenever they both had time off, they'd go dancing. 'We'd go up to London to the Hammersmith Palais, the Royal Opera House dance hall at Covent Garden, all the well-known dance halls. We had fun, laughed at the same things. We'd try to be together as often as we could.'

At the time, Biggin Hill had new arrivals: pilots from the United States Army Air Corps had been posted there to gain tactical experience. One of these pilots had offered Betty a flight in a Miles Magister. Yet it turned out he'd taken her up with the sole intention of giving her a bumpy ride and making her sick. When they got down and Betty realized his ruse, she'd promptly given him a swift kick in the shins before charging off. Word soon got round, thanks to Betty. As a result, she was given a nickname: 'Butch'. She was very much a no nonsense sort of girl.

That autumn, Joe's squadron was moved to Hornchurch in Essex. The WAAFs went with them. 'It was an exceptionally busy time on the flying side. I remember visits from Al Deere, who was Wing Commander of 611 Squadron at the time at Biggin Hill. He'd visit in a fancy Spitfire with all the rivet heads smoothed flush. The whole plane was polished like a cap badge. He said it definitely made the Spitfire go faster.'

Joe's friendship with Betty grew stronger. Yet their time together was abruptly cut short. 'It was decided to stand the air crew down for a rest period of three months, a break from operational flying. Some aircrew plus three ground crew were moved up to Drem, in North Berwick in Scotland, and I was one of them. The other ground crew were to remain behind at Hornchurch, along with Betty!'

By February 1944, it was time for 485 Squadron to move down south again. 'Typically, Betty had been posted north to Inverness and we were on our way back to Hornchurch.' But by the time Joe returned to Hornchurch, 485 Squadron were due to become part of the preparations for D-Day. The unit started to be much more mobile, as would be needed once they were shipped over to France post-invasion. 'It wasn't long before we were on the move again, this time to North Wales for gunnery and bombing practice. There was a lot of flying – the pilots were ready for it after a rest and we had our own squadron Spitfires back again. After two weeks, we were back at Hornchurch but not for long – our next move was to Selsey Advanced Landing Ground, near Chichester, in preparation for the invasion of Europe.'

By April 1944, these preparations were well underway. Air and ground crew would need to operate with minimum support and be asked to move at a moment's notice. Around Chichester, the air space was becoming crowded with squadrons operating from Tangmere, Ford, Merston, Apuldram, Funtington and Bognor. Accommodation was basic for ground crew and pilots alike. They were living under canvas. 'The whole squadron seemed to sense that for us, our part in the war had really come alive. The pilots were continually airborne, the weather was good and we were all pleased to be under canvas. It was an easier lifestyle in tents. We were much closer to the aircraft. A few yards to walk and you were at your Spitfire, which was very convenient.'

Time off, however, was virtually unheard of other than

the occasional twenty-four or forty-eight hour pass. 'I thought I'd never see Betty again. She was up in Inverness, although her home was in Worthing, not too far from me in Selsey. One day, while on leave, she'd visited me at Selsey. Unfortunately, that day I was away on some job or other, but she did send me a letter asking if I could possibly meet her at Worthing. I managed to get a twenty-four-hour pass and she met me at the station.'

Yet the reunion was to be brief – and bittersweet. 'She told me that her fiancé had arrived back in the UK and would be with her in a few days.' Joe was crestfallen. But he was determined to play fair, do the right thing. Hadn't he promised himself he'd be a gentleman? 'I couldn't get involved here. The situation was emotional and I'd given her my word that I would respect her engagement. I wasn't about to spoil it all now.' Betty wanted to go to the tea dance at Worthing Town Hall. 'We had just one dance, our favourite, a slow foxtrot. When I came to leave her at Worthing Station, she became very emotional and left in tears. "That's it," I thought to myself. "I'll never see her again."'

Although Joe believed his time with Betty had come to an end, there was no time to dwell on it, with a war to win and a day-to-day life that was always changing. Even working as ground staff had changed so much since he'd joined in 1939. 'At first they were all British pilots but as it progressed and the other countries got involved, Canadian, New Zealanders, Aussies, all sorts of nationalities, the atmosphere between the pilots and ground staff started to be different. In those first few months, all the pilots came from well-to-do families. You never initiated conversation.

When he landed you knew what to do, but then you were pushed out of the way. You just heard "Wipe the windscreen", "Fill the oil" and they'd go away. But once the auxiliaries and the reservists came in, it changed. They started chatting. As more experienced pilots came to us, things got better. And when the New Zealanders came with 485 Squadron, it was very informal. They were different – you were all on first name terms. So 485 became "our" Squadron.

'With D-Day, we knew we were going, we were even given French phrase books, everything you needed to know. The night before the invasion hundreds of gliders and paratroopers went ahead of the fighters, so the Spits could be the leading light in D-Day. We were still at Selsey Airfield the night before and my Squadron, 485, moved to Tangmere, twenty miles away. I went with an advance party in a Dakota from Tangmere and landed at Carpiquet, a few miles away from Caen. We just got on the job and forgot everything else, except what we were going to have to eat. You can't fight a war on an empty stomach.'

Joe and 485 Squadron saw a great deal of action right the way through to VE Day in 1945. For the rest of his life, he would always wear his squadron badge with pride: *Ka whawhai tonu* which is Maori for 'We will fight on'. In July 1945, with the war over, Joe got married to Mary, a pretty girl he'd met at an Army dance in Emsworth. It was time to settle down.

Almost a year later, in May 1946, he left the RAF and completed a two-year apprenticeship with a Sheffield engineering company as a machine tool maker and setter. In 1947, Joe and Mary had their first child, Kathleen Mary. But postwar housing in Sheffield was tricky for young marrieds and the pair decided that by Joe returning to the RAF, they'd have decent married quarters at least. So Joe rejoined in November 1948 as a leading aircraftsman engine fitter.

Yet again, Joe was in the thick of it with the Berlin Airlift, where the Russians had blocked all Allied access to divided Berlin, in an attempt to have complete control of the city. The RAF flew more than 200,000 flights in a year delivering fuel and food to the people trapped in Berlin's Western sector until the blockade ended. Joe worked long hours in Abingdon, Oxfordshire, on aircraft used in the Airlift, working mostly on the Rolls-Royce engines. Then he was despatched to Germany to work on aircraft there. As a consequence, he volunteered for a tour in Germany and Mary and the baby joined him there for three years. Back home, they had another child, Joseph Martin, in 1954, and Joe remained with the RAF until 1965, when he went to work at the Rolls-Royce aero engine department at Derby. He retired in 1982, aged sixty-one. 'We had a lovely home in Derby and I had plenty of hobbies: DIY, caravanning, fishing, you name it. Then my kids grew up and left home, so it was Mary, me and the dog rattling around in a three-bed semi.'

Life was good until 2000 when Mary was diagnosed with an inoperable brain tumour. She died in May 2001. Joe, typically, soldiered on afterwards, He'd maintained many of his Spitfire friendships from wartime, especially Spitfire pilot Bob Doe (Wing Commander Bob Doe, DSO, DFC and Bar) whom Joe knew from their far-off Battle of Britain days, as well as 485 Squadron's Doug Brown from Auckland, New Zealand. There were reunions, RAF events, many opportunities to revisit those times – and the enduring Spitfire memories they shared.

In 2004, Joe was interviewed for a Channel 4 documentary, *Spitfire Ace*. A few weeks after the documentary had been screened, a letter dropped onto his mat. It was from Betty. She now lived in Selsey, West Sussex, in a flat on her own. Her husband, Laurie Drury, had died some years earlier. She might easily have missed the programme had it not been for her grandson, Lawrence, who'd known something of Betty's wartime history and rang her to tell her about it. 'Watch it, Gran,' he'd told her. 'You were involved with Spitfires, weren't you?' Betty watched the documentary intently. She'd been amazed to see Joe up there on the screen. 'I know him!' she told her family. 'We used to go dancing!'

Nonetheless, she wasn't sure she should make contact. All those years; would he still be the same? After a bit of persuasion, she got in touch with Channel 4, explained who she was and, in due course, received Joe's address. Joe was astonished to receive her letter. 'I sat on it for about two weeks and then phoned her one evening. After a few phone calls, I said I wanted to visit her in Selsey.'

And so it was, sixty years later, that the twenty-something dance partners were reunited again. On another railway platform. 'I arrived at Chichester one afternoon by train. Betty was at the platform, waiting. It was magic, she was the same Betty to me as I'd last seen on that platform at Worthing sixty years earlier. I stayed with her for a couple of days and met the family and friends. I was reluctant to return to Derby.'

Two more visits to Selsey followed, each one longer than

the last. 'Then I asked how she'd feel about me moving down to live with her.' Betty was all for it. Joe, now eighty-three, promptly put his house up for sale, complete with contents, threw his Ford Escort in for good measure and got his asking price. He'd finally won the heart of his Betty, the golden girl he believed he'd lost. 'It was the start of eight of the most wonderful years of my life,' he recalled later. 'We didn't do much dancing although she could still trip the light fantastic all day, if you let her.'

After a few years, Betty sold her flat and the pair moved into a bungalow in Selsey. 'It was perfect. We lived life to the full, went on great holidays to Portugal, Isle of Wight, France, Wales. We even appeared on TV documentaries about the Battle of Britain with David Jason and one about Spitfires with John Sergeant. We were very, very happy.' Sadly, their happiness together ended in 2012. Betty died in Chichester hospital at the age of ninety-one, following emergency surgery on a ruptured stomach ulcer. 'I never thought I would lose her by outliving her – she was so strong and active,' Joe said afterwards.

Joe carried his sadness with him but he kept busy, still involved with aviation, a VIP guest at many events, even doing a parachute jump for charity at ninety. A year later, he was asked by Boultbee Flying Academy to start and run up their Mark IX Spitfire. In front of the waiting crowd at Goodwood, he fired up the Merlin – at one of the many airfields he'd served with 485 Squadron back in 1943.

He died at home on 19 April 2017, just days before his ninety-sixth birthday.

## FORGOTTEN HEROES

In 2012, Squadron Leader Doug Brown of the Royal New Zealand Air Force (1919–2013) wrote of his admiration for the ground crews who serviced the Spitfires and other planes for 485 Squadron from 1941 to 1945:

> Unlike the Spitfire pilots in the squadron, who were in the main New Zealanders, this was not the case for the ground crew. Many of the ground crew personnel, including Joe Roddis, were with the squadron for the duration until it was disbanded in 1945. As pilots, we were so very dependent on the ground crew and close associations were formed. The ground crew regularly serviced aircraft through the night to ensure that they were operational.
>
> Squadrons usually had eighteen aircraft. A standard service took about twenty-four hours. In addition, damaged planes required a higher level of service and new planes underwent a complete commissioning process. The work backlog was consequently high. The dedication and effort put in by the ground crew was not appreciated by the population at large.
>
> The New Zealand pilots by their nature enjoyed the company of the ground crew. There was a rapport quite unlike that of other squadrons. They were treated as equals by commanding officer and pilots alike. When misdemeanours were committed (contrary to regulation and brought to account by

the hierarchy!) we, as pilots, would ensure there were no grounds to pursue.

As pilots, while we flew the Spitfires, without the dedication and enthusiastic support of the ground crew our operational flying would have been badly impaired due to a lack of confidence in the reliability of our aircraft, whether it be engine, oxygen, radio or armament. They were the forgotten heroes!

## Wanted: One Handsome Pilot

Two weeks before D-Day, in May 1944, a group of four ATA female pilots were flying over the Solent in a taxi plane. Down below, they could easily see the huge preparations for the Normandy invasion: landing craft already on the Solent, waiting there for the big day. Then one of the girls had a bright idea.

'Since there were going to be lots of men around the landing craft, she said why didn't we try putting a message in a bottle, with our names and where we could be found?' recalled Mary Ellis, one of the group. 'That way, some handsome chap would pick up the message and come and find us. How stupid we were! We laughed and threw the bottles out of the air taxi, as close to the landing craft as we could. But of course it was really a silly distraction for us, a release from tension if you like.'

Yet the message in a bottle incident was not Mary's only attempt to attract the attention of a handsome beau.

After D-Day, another opportunity came along. 'On 15 September I had to deliver a brand-new Mark VIII Spitfire from Eastleigh, near Southampton, to RAF Brize Norton in Oxfordshire. While I was waiting for the taxi plane to come and collect me, I decided to leave my mark, yet again. So I wrote my name in pencil "Flight Officer Mary Wilkins [her maiden name], ATA" on the inside of the cockpit in the hope that some handsome RAF fighter pilot would see it. And my message would, in time, be discovered.' But this didn't happen in the way Mary hoped it would.

Nearly twenty years later, and Mary had been happily married to a handsome, charming pilot, Donald Ellis, for several years. By then, she was running Sandown Airport on the Isle of Wight, a thriving business with commercial planes flying in holidaymakers from all over the UK. 'In January 1980, a vintage warbird man, Robs Lamplough, got in touch with us. He told us he had just imported a Spitfire MV 154 from Australia. The plane had been assembled in 1960 in Australia but never flown as the then owner could not get permission to fly it. Instead, the owner had suspended it from the roof in his hangar and there it had remained, unopened and untouched for two decades.

'When the owner died, Robs was able to buy the aircraft from the deceased's estate. Imagine his amazement upon getting the plane back in the UK, opening the cockpit to find … my name written in the cockpit!' According to the plane's logbook, Mary had flown that Spitfire for twenty-five minutes – and it turned out she had been the only person to fly it. 'You were often the test pilot when you made the delivery,' she recalled.

For some reason, after Mary's delivery in September 1944, the plane had gone around the different war zones and wound up in Australia in November that year, still in its crate from being shipped from England. After a great deal of work and a replacement engine, the plane flew again in the summer of 1992. 'Of course we went to see it and the story of me writing my name, hoping to find my handsome pilot, caused much laughter with Robs and his family. Because in the end, I did find him.'

## Jack and Peggy

It was the summer of 1940 and WAAF (Women's Auxiliary Air Force) Peggy Balfour was stationed at RAF Digby in Lincolnshire. She had been posted there in September 1939.

Twenty-three-year-old Peggy was an Operations Room Plotter, one of a team of WAAFs working in the station's Ops Room, where the operations of all the fighters were monitored. Plotting was, essentially, an early form of air traffic control. The work involved monitoring all available information about the aircraft, using magnetized plotting rods to move around counters positioned on a giant table bearing a map of the section, and changing the plots regularly so an entire picture of a raid could be monitored by the Group Controller.

Peggy enjoyed her job and the RAF social life, usually dances held in the Sergeants' Mess. And it was at one of these dances that she met Jack 'Farmer' Lawson, a fighter pilot from 46 Squadron, then based at RAF Digby. Peggy kept a diary. She wrote: 'What joy! He was tall and I found he danced beautifully.' They got to know each other well. 'We used to visit the local pubs or buy fish and chips and eat them out of newspaper. The weather always seemed to be fine and sunny. We laughed a lot and were always talking. We talked about everything and we argued – we certainly did not agree all the time. I remember he was always teasing me about my ideas and I think he thought me a little mad. But we enjoyed our jaunts into the countryside. We had lots of fun and, best of all, Jack never fussed.' Jack was posted to 19 Squadron just before the Battle of Britain began in July. They regularly exchanged letters and occasionally, Jack would fly to RAF Digby to visit Peggy.

In January 1941, Peggy was posted to RAF Duxford to work in the Operations Room. By then, Jack was a Flight Lieutenant, commanding 19 Squadron's 'A' flight. The day before her posting was announced, she wrote in her diary: 'If I should go anywhere – could it be Duxford, just could I be so lucky? What shall I do without my friends? Of course if I went to Duxford I should have Jack somewhere around – would that be a good thing, would I know too much? Whatever happens, I must not seem too gloomy. There is enough of that around at the moment.'

Peggy soon got used to life at Duxford. She found she could not always see Jack as he was often scrambled to fly combat missions. But they spent many happy days together in nearby Cambridge. One of her fondest memories was of the day Jack came into the Operations Room and acted as Controller, with Peggy as his assistant. She also remembered the time Jack had flown her to a dance in his Spitfire. In a very cramped cockpit in a one-seater fighter aircraft, the only way she could have travelled with him was by sitting on his lap – surely something the authorities would have frowned upon, had they ever found out.

On 30 August 1941, Peggy wrote in her diary: 'I mustn't give in, I must write something down in my diary, but what can I say? Just that Jack has been shot down. He is missing, there is no hope for him; 19 Squadron are searching for remnants this morning.' Peggy clung onto the hope that Jack had survived, but sadly her hope was in vain. Jack had been shot down and killed over Rotterdam on 28 August. The only memento that Peggy had of Jack Lawson was a sketch that she had drawn, years later, from memories of Jack.

After he was killed, Peggy was posted to the RAF's Photographic Unit at the No. 1 School of Photography, No. 24 Group. Yet she never forgot her beloved Jack. She remained single for the rest of her life, maintaining her links with the WAAF.

In 1998, collections staff at RAF Duxford were able to give Peggy a video of RAF Duxford during the Second World War. It included moving footage of Jack Lawson. She also received photographs of Jack – the first she had seen in fifty-seven years. The following year, she revisited IWM Duxford with a group of WAAF veterans who had served in the Operations Room at nearby Sawston Hall, which controlled the fighters going into combat from RAF Duxford.

Peggy died in July 2000, aged eighty-two.

## 'FARMER' JACK

Squadron Leader Walter John 'Jack' Lawson was born in 1913. He joined the RAF as an apprentice and initially worked as an aircraft fitter before completing his training as a pilot. He joined 19 Squadron in April 1940. His nickname on the squadron was 'Farmer' as he often spoke of plans to become one after the war. On 5 September 1940, he was appointed Flight Commander and was awarded the DFC (Distinguished Flying Cross) in November 1940, having destroyed at least five enemy aircraft. In June 1941, he shot down and destroyed two further aircraft.

On 28 August 1941, he failed to return from a Circus offensive (a large formation of Blenheim bombers heavily escorted by sixteen fighters to Rotterdam in order to draw enemy fighters into combat) while flying off the Dutch coast in his Spitfire IIA P7995. He was twenty-eight years old.

## Pat and Kay

On Saturday, 7 September 1940, dawn was breaking as Kay Hughes set off in her car on the long journey from St Eval, Cornwall to Andover, Hampshire. She was sad to leave the pretty seaside house where she and Pat, her husband of just thirty-seven days, should have spent their honeymoon. But in the end, they'd had their wedding night in a hotel in Newquay and Pat, an Australian fighter pilot, had spent hardly any time at RAF St Eval, the strategic RAF station where he'd been briefly located with 234 Squadron that fateful summer of the Battle of Britain.

Pat Hughes had been with the RAF for two years. At twenty-two, he was a fearless Spitfire pilot, Squadron leader in all but name of 234 Squadron. Kay had met him in February 1940 in the Beverley Arms, near Leconfield and her home in Hull. The daughter of a widowed mother, Kay Brodrick was a pretty girl, if a bit spoilt. She had her own car, nice clothes and was never short of a boyfriend. But she thought the fair-haired Aussie was outstanding from the moment he'd walked into the pub: tall with grey eyes, he was carrying an Airedale puppy he'd named 'Flying Officer Butch'. Pat loved flying and Britain, even though he missed his family back home. And, in a short space of time, he would also fall in love with Kay. 'The war will be over in a year,' he told her as he put the diamond engagement ring on her finger two months later in April.

But May brought Dunkirk and by July he'd been posted to St Eval. He phoned Kay to say: 'Let's not waste any more time, darling, we can get married at Bodmin Register Office.' They were married there on 1 August 1940.

After that, there were only brief moments of happiness in between Pat's demanding and exhausting fighter-attack sorties. On one occasion, Pat managed twenty-four hours leave, just the two of them – and Flying Officer Butch, who by now was reputed to have had more flying hours in Spitfires than some pilots. 'One day it'll always be like this,' he promised. 'Just you, me and another Flying Officer Butch – I mean if we ever have a son.' But mostly, married life for Kay meant waiting in the lonely seaside house in

St Eval – until Pat was suddenly moved to RAF Middle Wallop, Andover. 'We're on the move again,' he said on the phone. 'Lock up the house and get to the White Hart, Andover. Be there, now.'

On 16 August, Pat's plane had been badly shot up. He'd missed death by inches. That night he joked: 'In case of accidents, make sure you marry again.' Within days, Kay noticed, the pilots in Pat's squadron seemed to have gone from boys to men. Sometimes they seemed very tired. But never fed up.

On Thursday, 5 September, Pat told her there was so much going on, he thought it would be better if Kay went home to Hull for a while. 'Okay but I'll have to fetch our things from Cornwall first, drive up to Andover and we'll stay at the White Hart on Saturday night,' Kay told him. Everyone wanted a room at the White Hart, but Pat and Kay had snatched all but one of their eleven married nights together there, so the landlord promised he'd keep a double room for them.

On the Friday, Kay had made the long drive down to Cornwall, packed that night and all day, a beautiful sunny Saturday, she drove up to Hampshire. Kay was a few miles from Andover when she found a phone box and rang the Mess, asking for Pat.

But instead, she got the fatherly adjutant, 'Bish'. 'Come right over, Kay, I'll meet you at the gate,' he said. Clutching the gold charm bracelet Pat had given her, Kay knew what was to come. Bish and some of the boys took her to the White Hart when she arrived. The landlord beamed: 'I've got your double'.

'Pat had bailed out, but a German fighter followed him down, riddling him with bullets. It must have been over in seconds, they said,' Kay recalled in 1980. 'I asked if I could have Flying Officer Butch to take home with me, but that afternoon he'd run out of the Mess. They never found him.'

A week after Pat's funeral in Sutton-on-Hull, Yorkshire, Kay discovered she was pregnant. 'I was glad, but I still couldn't stop crying,' she said. Then, at nearly four months, she miscarried. It was a boy. 'After that, I didn't care about anything except getting drunk and playing Pat's favourite record, "Where or When", tears streaming down.'

When Hull was bombed, she drove a converted ambulance. Then she went into the WAAF. Pat was awarded a posthumous DFC. 'The King gave it to me. Other widows were crying. I wasn't. Every tear had poured out in 1940.'

After the war, Kay remarried. 'Pat told me to marry again, so I did. In 1946 I met an Army officer, an ex-prisoner of war. We had three or four happy years, two lovely sons. Then disaster set in. He left the country and, penniless, I had to divorce him.'

After that there was a third marriage. Again, it ended in divorce. Then Kay worked for many years as the matron of an old people's home, a job she enjoyed very much.

She had already retired when she met her fourth husband, also widowed. 'We married for companionship. He understands, so do my sons, that when I die, I want my ashes put with Pat. It's always been in my will. I've an idea that the first person I will meet will be Pat, not grown old or changed at all. I don't know what he'll make of me, but he'll understand everything, just as he always did, and we'll have time together, at last.'

Kay died on 28 June 1983, aged sixty-six. Exactly as she wished, her ashes were buried with her beloved Pat in St James Churchyard, Sutton-on Hull, Yorkshire.

## SOMETHING SPECIAL

Paterson Clarence Hughes, known as Pat, was born in 1917 in the Monaro region, a pastoral and mining area at the foot of New South Wales' Snowy Mountains. He was one of eleven children, his parents' youngest son. He loved sport, surf and his greatest youthful joy was making model aeroplanes out of balsa wood. By his late teens, he applied for and was offered a cadetship at the Royal Australian Air Force's training school at Point Cook, near Melbourne, Victoria. He completed his pilot training in November 1936.

Pat decided to join the RAF when he finished his cadetship as he wanted to 'try and do something special'. Following additional training in England, he was initially posted to 64 Squadron in June 1937 and in November 1939 he was posted to the newly formed 234 Squadron as a flight commander.

Pat was a natural-born good shot. He developed an uncompromising combat style, believing in getting as close to the enemy as possible. He was known for opening fire at 100 yards, closing to 50 or less. It was highly dangerous and, indeed, his Spitfire was hit on many occasions. He was also the driving force behind 234 Squadron. When morale was low, he raised everyone's spirits. In the air he was tough and focused. But on the ground he remained 'one of the boys'.

Between 13 August and 7 September, 234 Squadron shot down sixty-three enemy aircraft, fighting to the point of exhaustion. In the final week of his life, Pat carried out twelve sorties in seven days and was in battle again on 7 September, the first day of the London Blitz. He thrust his Spitfire towards a formation of Dornier Do 17s and picked out a straggler. His machine-gun fire was so concentrated, a large piece fell off. One of the wings then crumpled and the stricken aircraft fell into a fatal spin.

Pat bailed out as his Spitfire plummeted, too, but no one knows if it had been hit by enemy fire, knocked by falling debris or if the aggressive pilot had deliberately rammed the Dornier. His parachute failed to open. On a blazing blue autumn evening twelve days before his twenty-third birthday, he fell to his death in a suburban garden in Bessels Green, Kent.

He accrued 14 confirmed, 3 shared, 1 probable and 1 unconfirmed enemy planes destroyed, the highest-scoring Australian fighter pilot in the Battle of Britain. Later he was ranked in the top ten Battle of Britain pilots and in the RAF's top 50. In going to England he had undeniably done 'something special'.

# CHAPTER 7

# Afterwards

IN THE TWENTY-FIRST CENTURY, DECADES after the end of the war, the story of the Spitfire lives on. An icon of the war, its enduring legacy continues to touch lives at home and abroad. From myths surrounding what may have happened to some of the aircraft that were decommissioned after the war, to their use in rehabilitating and inspiring badly injured servicemen, to the wonderful airshows that they take part in throughout the country every year, the Spitfire is second to none in British military history as a symbol of hope and victory.

## The Oakey Legend

At the end of the Second World War, Australia was home to thousands of military aircraft, machines that had become surplus to Australia's postwar needs. Hundreds of aircraft were sent to aircraft depots all over the country to be turned back into components or scrapped and melted down. One of these was No. 6 Aircraft Depot (6AD) at Oakey, in Queensland, just 100 miles west of one of Australia's largest cities, Brisbane.

Royal Australian Air Force records show that by mid-1946, 554 fighter planes, including Mustangs, Kittyhawks and Boomerangs, were sent to Oakey for disposal; 232 of these were Spitfires. But what happened to them? The Oakey Spitfires became, over time, the subject of fierce speculation in Australia evolving into what many call the Oakey Legend, the belief that many crated Spitfires were buried, either in mine shafts, tunnels or pits, by those determined to preserve them.

Documentary filmmakers James Carter and Karl von Moller have notched up twenty years researching the fate of the Oakey Spitfires. They are firmly convinced that the legend is very far from myth. 'Apart from the people of Oakey, everyone from local historians, historical societies and aircraft enthusiasts as well as current Australian Defence Force Personnel from the Australian Army and Air Force all know about the buried Spitfires. Not every story we have researched has been exactly the same but what is amazing is that they're all pretty close,' said James Carter.

At first the Spitfires at Oakey were put up for sale. 'There were public auctions around 1946/7 and they took place on the site at Oakey – but no one was interested. Some of the engines were sold to commercial dealers and there was outcry for a while about what the government was doing with these wonderful planes. In the end, the Ministry of Air decided to put them through their disposal commission, tasked to get rid of them. A scrap metal company, a consortium based in the nearby town of Toowoomba, took on the contract. But the company underestimated the time it would take to dispose of the aircraft – and they had a contractual deadline. They set up a smelter on site and the aircraft were then turned into ingots of aluminium. Most of them were chopped up, a few taken away to be used for training of fitters. But an undetermined quantity of aircraft pieces were believed to have been thrown into disused coal mine shafts or nearby rubbish tips by the disposal gangs.'

Personnel still working at the Oakey Depot at the end of the war, they just wanted to get the job done quickly and go home. For their part, there was a major imperative to clear out everything in the hangars. Stories have circulated that these men witnessed truckloads of equipment in boxes and crates leaving the Oakey base to be dumped somewhere in the region, perhaps in an area called Kingsthorpe, 5 km from Oakey where a number of coal mines and shafts are located. 'We went there and found all these Spitfire undercarriage legs sitting there, beside the old shaft,' said James Carter. 'So the stories of parts being thrown down the old coal mines to get rid of them were true.'

But the stories of crated Spitfires, rather than parts, being put down into mines are more complicated. 'The size of the mines in that area – and most in Queensland – are not big enough to take a crated Spit. But one mine, the Federal Mine, located off the main street of Oakey, near the Council Depot, close to the town and the Oakey Depot, had tunnels as well as shafts, tunnels larger than others in the area. So the little rail tracks into the mine could have been used.' Spitfire-obsessed locals have made sporadic attempts to dig in the Federal Mine area, but such attempts have failed.

There are many theories as to why the Oakey Spitfires may have been buried in the area after the war. The most extreme is that they were a stockpile for the years after their burial, in case of a nuclear attack on Australia. But the most credible theory surrounds the men working at the base. 'They'd just lived through the Second World War. After six years, all they wanted was to go home, go back to their families and get their lives back on track. It was tantalizingly close. The only thing stopping them was clearing out the base. The quickest way to fix that was to dump the aircraft and leftover parts anywhere they could.'

## ONE FOR POSTERITY

John Marshall was born in 1948. His father, Walter Neville Marshall, known as 'Nev', was stationed at Oakey airbase during the Second World War. He was employed by the Royal Australian Air Force as a flight mechanic/aircraft fitter before being demobbed, in 1946, aged nineteen. 'My father worked on engines, airframes, repairs, modifications, he was there for about three years or so. I must have been about five years old when I remember him telling me bedtime stories about how he and his mates buried a crated Spitfire at Oakey. Dad told me he and his mates dug a hole big enough to take a crated Spitfire and a couple of fuel drums. There were a couple of trees at the front of the hole and they used a gantry to lift the crate into the hole. They dug, with great difficulty, by hand, over the course of about three weeks, but it was all done undercover. There was only one crate involved. He said it was a Spitfire Mark 8 that was buried.'

The stories stayed with John Marshall. Aviation became, as he grew up, a bit of a passion. 'In the seventies, I learned to fly. About that time there were press reports about the buried Spits at Oakey and that triggered the memories of Dad's stories.'

In 1982, John encouraged his father to accompany him on a trip to Oakey, just to see if they could retrieve any useful information about Nev's memories of the buried plane. 'Dad was able to identify certain landmarks around the base, like the water tower and he was able to go straight to the place where he thought they had buried the Spits on the southern perimeter of the base. During that visit we also had contact with a local farmer and went for a drive-by of a few landmarks. There had been some digging in the Oakey area that year but a few years later it came to a grinding halt.'

What really convinced John Marshall that his father's stories were true was their consistency: they never changed at all over the years. 'We had dinner together many times and went back to the story over and over again. There was a consistent thread all the time. Dad told me the crated Spit came into the hangar with a number of other crates at the end of 1945. I assume it came in by rail and was crated over to the base. After they'd buried it, no one showed any interest about whether it was missing. Everyone was waiting to get demobbed. Dad told me while he was on guard duty one night, three semi-trailers took other crated aircraft out of the base. He was on guard roster, midnight to 6 a.m. He recalled three semi-trailers with five crates leaving the base, turning left, heading east. The trailers were away for about three and a half hours, back at the base at 6 a.m. He saw this but was not involved personally. I suspect the five crates on the semi-trailers were destined for a mine shaft, not above ground.'

Nev Marshall died in November 1997, aged seventy. 'Like every young pilot, I wanted to fly a Spitfire over the Oakey base. Dad was what we call a "scallywag" – he loved the footy, he was a man's man, he had a great sense of humour. I don't think for one minute this was a story concocted to tell a five-year-old boy. It was done to expedite their demob. He told me: "We put one down for posterity."'

## Sergeant Robinson's Dream

Alan Robinson looked up at the consultant standing by his hospital bed. He could see the obvious concern on the man's face. He was about to deliver the bad news. But Alan already knew what was coming. The night before, in the ambulance, he'd been warned of the possible consequences of the accident he'd just had on his motorbike. A motorist, overtaking another car, had unexpectedly come onto Alan's side of the road – and almost wiped him out for good.

'It was a serious accident,' he said of the night in 2011 when his life changed for good. 'I'd severed an artery in the crash and lost a lot of blood. I remained conscious until I got to hospital, but the next morning I woke up, looked down and could only see one foot under the covers. I knew I'd lost a leg, just below the knee. It was a shock, even though they'd already warned me they might have to amputate. At the time, it didn't fully register just how different things would be.'

Alan had joined the RAF in 1998. An aircraft engineer, based at RAF Waddington, it had been his ambition, since childhood, to sign up and train as a pilot. But a family crisis when Alan was taking his 'O' Levels had led to a change of heart. 'So I joined as an aircraft technician, as ground crew. A job I've always enjoyed.'

Adjusting to the shock of his disability was never going to be straightforward or easy. But after his accident, he tried his best to remain rational. 'As someone with an engineering background, I'm quite a logical thinker. So I thought: "Let's take this one stage at a time."' Until the accident, much of his spare time after work had been taken up with his passion for racing motorbikes. Now, of course, this was out of the question. But as the months passed and he started to recover, Alan realized he wanted to challenge himself. Would flying, once his childhood dream, be possible? He already had a friend flying microlights. Could that somehow be an option? 'I researched it and just a few days from getting my prosthetic leg, I was flying near Salisbury at Old Sarum Airfield,' he recalled.

Alan had got involved with a charity called Flying for Freedom (partnered by the charity Help for Heroes) which helps disabled people still in rehabilitation into recovery, supporting them through microlight flying training. Microlights are open-cockpit 'weight shift' aircraft, one of the easiest and cheapest ways to fly. Training to fly one offers basic air experience but it also provides an exhilarating adventure. This chance to fly proved to be immensely liberating for Alan. 'Thanks to Flying for Freedom, I got my microlight pilot's licence – and I realized straight away that the best thing about it all was up there in an aircraft, I was no longer a disabled person.'

It looked like he'd found the perfect way to reconcile himself to his disability. But in 2013, Alan heard about something that really made him think hard: a scholarship of a most unusual kind. A Spitfire Scholarship.

Run by Matt Jones, Managing Director of the Boultbee Flight Academy at Goodwood Aerodrome, with the assistance of the Royal Foundation's Endeavour Fund and, specifically, HRH Prince Harry, the new two-year Spitfire Scholarship was set up to train two wounded, sick and injured military personnel, with very little aviation experience, to fly the iconic plane.

The first step was a selection meeting at RAF Cranwell for some tests and a flying assessment. 'There were some extremely talented candidates attending the Officers & Aircrew Selection Centre at Cranwell but Alan stood out right from the start,' remembers Matt Jones of the day Alan was awarded the Scholarship along with Private Nathan Forster, who'd lost part of his leg in an IED (improvised explosive device) blast in 2011 in Afghanistan, while serving with the Parachute Regiment. Alan was thrilled beyond belief. 'I probably smiled for a week after that.'

The Spitfire Scholarship involved two years' training, a total of sixty flying hours, using wartime aircraft and training techniques. Training was split with thirty hours flying a de Havilland Chipmunk, twenty on a Harvard, then, finally, ten hours on a Spitfire. To take part, Alan had to progress from his microlight pilot's licence to a light aircraft private pilot's licence. He passed this initial test in a Cessna C152, then moved onto training on the Chipmunk. Around this time he got his first real look at a Spitfire at Boultbee. 'The first time I saw it in the hangar I was startled by it, the most beautiful airplane that will ever be made. Yet actually flying it, then, still felt beyond a dream for me.'

None of the aircraft used in the Scholarship for training were modified to compensate for Alan or Nathan's prosthetic limbs. Nonetheless, Alan's dedication to the challenges ahead of him became increasingly obvious as he trained. 'He flew with us relentlessly for two summers, building his knowledge and skills,' explains Matt Jones. 'His ability was never in doubt and he continued to show a talent far above average while together we sought solutions to the challenges presented by having only one leg. Interestingly, the greatest obstacles in this respect came from flying the training aircraft, the Chipmunk and the Harvard, rather than the Spitfire itself.'

'At times, with the Chipmunk, it was as though I was trying to pat my head and rub my tummy. I worried that I really wasn't getting it,' Alan admitted later. But sure enough, those initial concerns gradually faded away each time he took to the skies for his training. The Spitfire training was in an original single seat Mark IX, the last Spitfire mark to be flown with the RAF until June 1957. 'It had entered RAF service in May 1945,' explained Alan. 'It never saw combat and later it was converted into a twin-seater. My training regime was quite similar to how it would have been back then. I was worried I might not be able to cope with the Spitfire. For the first three or four hours it was just the sheer speed and power of it. I couldn't keep up after flying the Harvard and that's a reasonably fast plane. Of course, the reality of the Spitfire was difficult, and a bit of a knock to my confidence. But once we were a few hours further down the road and I started to get a feel for it, I began to get used to it.'

Finally, the last weekend of October 2016 dawned. Alan was due to make his solo flight on the last Sunday of the month at Lee-on-Solent Airfield (once the main training establishment of the Fleet Air Arm) overlooking the Solent and the Isle of Wight. 'On the Saturday there was a bit of uncertainty around the weather, so I had all Saturday night to think about it. But on the Sunday, when I got to the airfield, the excitement was tangible. About a hundred people were there – a big group of people involved in restoring aircraft. My wife, Louise, and my little boy, Thomas, who's four, were at home [in Market Rasen, Lincolnshire] unfortunately. That was the only downside.'

Alan tried to shield himself from the excitement around him as the big moment approached. 'I just had to concentrate on the job in hand. First, I did a couple of circuits with Matt and he assessed me.' At that point, the weather improved. Alan readied himself for his solo, ten-minute circuit. It went beautifully. The crowd clapped their approval. He'd done it. The first solo Spitfire flight to be made by an amputee since the war and the flights made by the legendary wartime heroes Douglas Bader and Colin

'Hoppy' Hopkinson. 'I was elated and gutted, too, that the scholarship was over. I wanted it to go on for ever, I was enjoying the adventure so much,' he recalled. 'I was on a massive high.'

'Seeing Alan go solo was no surprise to any of us that flew with him,' said Matt Jones. 'Not surprising. But very emotional.' Since then, Alan has been promoted to Sergeant and works in a technical advisory role for the RAF. He has also continued to pass on everything he learned through his scholarship experience. His involvement with Flying for Freedom and with other flying scholarships allows him to mentor other disabled candidates. 'Once your confidence builds and you get the hang of it, you start to see that it's not as difficult as you'd built it up in your mind. It's a case of knocking down the mental barriers.'

As for the Spitfire's links to the past, there is nothing but admiration for those that flew the Spit, defending the country. 'I feel a greater than ever respect for them, now I've had the privilege of meeting some of them. I hope to preserve their memories and stories for ever.'

## REACH FOR THE SKY

Group Captain Sir Douglas Bader, CBE, DSO and Bar, DFC and Bar, FRAeS, DL (1910–82) lost both legs in a flying accident in 1931. He went on to fly in the Battle of Britain and shot down twenty enemy aircraft before being shot down in France in 1941, ending the war as a POW in Colditz. His remarkable story was told in the BAFTA award-winning film *Reach for the Sky* starring Kenneth More. Bader campaigned passionately for the disabled and continued to fly almost until the end of his life.

Flight Lieutenant Colin 'Hoppy' Hopkinson (1920–96) also lost both legs in an accident while training with the Fleet Air Arm in 1939. Inspired by Bader's achievements, he transferred from the Royal Navy to the RAF, flying Spitfires for 131 Squadron. In April 1943, he shot down an Fw 190 which crashed into the sea at Brighton Pier, and a few months later he was posted to 611 Squadron where he claimed a second aerial victory in a dogfight following a bombing run in south-west France. In November 1943, he was on a reconnaissance mission over France when he crash-landed in a field. He was pulled from his burning Spitfire by farm workers, losing an artificial leg in the process. Held prisoner in POW camp Stalag Luft 111 until he was repatriated, his RAF career ended in 1946. After the war he ran a successful public relations business and retired to the Dordogne, France, a decade before he died.

## The Secret Party

Stella Broughton stared at the magnificent buffet in front of her. She couldn't quite believe her eyes. Five big trestle tables covered with spotlessly white cloths, groaning under the weight of a beautifully presented array of delicious food, the like of which had not been seen for a long time by most people in the country.

It was the summer of 1944 and twenty-year-old Stella, who worked in the Vickers Supermarine drawing office, had long grown accustomed to rationing and food shortages. This wasn't just a decent spread – it was positively lavish. Roast chicken, legs of lamb, roast beef, even a huge joint of roast pork. Fruit salad, jugs of cream, cakes, big bowls of every kind of fruit including bananas and oranges, rarely seen at the time. There were bottles of whisky, gin, wine, liqueurs, beer. Along a facing wall were musical instruments and stands for the musicians, gleaming cutlery and glasses, everything polished and buffed to perfection for a VIP party.

It had all started that morning, Saturday 3 June, as Stella sat at her drawing board. She'd been at the Vickers Supermarine drawing office at Hursley Park House, an eighteenth-century Queen Anne-style mansion in Winchester, for nearly three years. (Hursley House had been requisitioned by the Ministry of Aircraft Production to rehouse the Design and Production departments of Vickers Supermarine after it had been bombed out of its original premises at Woolston, Southampton.) Stella's work involved producing master copies from the drawings of the draughtsmen in her section, updated designs of the Spitfire, the Spiteful (a Rolls-Royce Griffon-engined fighter designed as a successor to the Spitfire in the latter part of the war) and other aircraft – top secret work enabling the production and assembly of new aircraft. It was well paid and Stella, the only woman in a team of 100 Supermarine draughtsmen, loved her job.

She'd been headhunted by Supermarine from her previous job in the experimental drawing office of

HMS *Excellent* at Whale Island, Portsmouth, and by now she was a valued, experienced member of the team, working out of the camouflaged Drawing Office in an underground aircraft hangar just beyond the gardens of Hursley House. She was, of course, proud of her role in the production of the Spitfire. 'Everyone knew the Spitfire was superior to anything the Germans had. The general attitude was: "We've got the Spitfire and we're going to beat Germany with it". That gave comfort to everyone, to know we had that wonderful plane.'

As for being the lone woman in what was essentially an all-male environment, this did not trouble her at all. 'I was older than some girls of my age in attitude and more knowledgeable,' she said. 'I could mix with people. My mother headed up various women's groups in the church so I'd go with her to church functions, attend meetings, serve tea with the ladies. Or go to all-male events with my father.' Yet nothing in Stella's past could have prepared her for what lay ahead.

Looking up from her drawing board that morning she spotted Joseph Smith, Supermarine's Chief Designer, accompanied by a military officer, making their way through the hangar. Then her boss, Gerry Gyngell, head of Technical Publications, stopped by her drawing board. Stella was wanted in Mr Lovell-Cooper's office (Eric Lovell-Cooper was the Chief Draughtsman). Knowing full well that many pairs of eyes in the big office had been alerted to her being summoned into the Chief Draughtsman's office, Stella made her way there. She was as curious as everyone else.

'Er … are you doing anything particular this afternoon?'

asked Mr Lovell-Cooper. Stella said no, she wasn't, did they want her to come in? Then she realized the military officer was sitting in the corner of the office. Joseph Smith had gone. She was introduced to the officer, Major General Douglas Graham. 'Would you be kind enough to accept an invitation to a party tonight?' he said, shaking her hand. 'I'd be delighted if you would honour me with your company as my personal guest. The party is for the opening of a new Officers' Mess at my HQ near Hursley House and I'd like you to act as my hostess.' Stella was taken aback by the request and her mind was racing. Hostess? What did that mean? In those days, the word had tricky connotations. Surely this was something much more serious? Either way, she felt she couldn't refuse. Even if she didn't have an evening dress. The General assured her that it wasn't a formal affair and there would be other ladies present, too: one who worked in the main house, and some other American ladies. 'I have a yellow day dress, it's an old gold colour,' Stella said helpfully. The General assured her that would be suitable, though when she said the words 'old gold' she thought she saw a brief flicker of apprehension cross his face.

It was all arranged. A jeep would come to her digs in Winchester to collect her at 7 p.m. The driver would have a special security pass to get her into the heavily guarded camp where the party would be held. 'What was that all about then?' asked one of her colleagues tentatively as Stella made her way back to the drawing board. 'Oh, I've been invited to a party,' she replied, knowing full well no one would enquire further. Their work was top secret – people knew better than to pry.

That evening, in her gold dress and the new matching gold velvet headband she'd managed to make, she made her first ever journey in an American jeep to the high security party location, a Nissen hut tucked away in the woods near Hursley House. On arrival, she was met by the Major General, who guided her to a secluded area for a confidential chat. Only then did she learn why she was there, though she'd already decided that the party was something more significant than she'd been told. She was right. In fact, the party was a prelude to the biggest secret of the Second World War thus far.

'We are close to D-Day,' Major General Graham told her. 'That's why you've been asked to be hostess this evening.' Codenamed 'Operation Overlord' and over a year in the planning, D-Day, also known as the Normandy landings, was the pivotal point in the war when the Allied forces made their combined naval, air and land assault on Nazi-occupied France to establish a foothold along the northern coast of France in order to begin their advance. Early on 6 June, Allied airborne forces would be parachuted into dropzones across Northern France. Ground troops would land across five assault beaches across a fifty-mile stretch of the Normandy coast, the beaches named Utah, Omaha, Juno, Sword and Gold – hence the General's somewhat apprehensive look when Stella had mentioned the colour of her dress. More than sixty of the most senior British and American military commanders taking part in Overlord and their staff were the party's guests, many meeting each other for the first time.

Stella's role, as directed from as high up as Generals

Eisenhower and Montgomery, was to help make the top-secret pre-D-Day party a success. Her presence, as both a civilian and a female would bring an element of normal life into the evening. She was to greet each guest, help them relax, talk briefly to them – without any mention of why they were there, of course.

The high level of security surrounding the planning of D-Day meant that not only was she now privy to the war's biggest secret: she could not, under any circumstances, reveal any information about the secret party until at least sixty years had passed. Because of the nature of her work, Stella, like her colleagues, had already been required to sign the Official Secrets Act for her drawing office job. Yet hosting the party itself placed her on the high security Bigot list (British Invasion of Occupied German Territory). An event like this eve of invasion party had never been held before any major battle. 'I was not intimidated,' recalled Stella, remembering the moment when she took in the enormity of her involvement. 'I was quite mature in my thinking. And I had two brothers, so I was used to male company, being at the forefront of a group of people.'

In any case, there wasn't time to deliberate or mull over what she'd been asked to do. Major General Graham, as the senior British Commanding Officer, was now greeting every guest as they came through the door. Soon he was bringing each man to be introduced to the pretty young English girl in the yellow dress. Stella had been told to spend between ten minutes or half an hour talking to each officer, helping them relax. They were introduced to her according to their rank but she sensibly chose to address each one as 'Mr', making pleasant, easy small talk about all manner of light topics, ushering them towards the refreshments, generally putting the men at ease by talking about holidays, gardens, flowers, trees, even musical concerts. Yet it was Stella's discretion and common sense that would be crucial in making the party run smoothly.

One officer brought in by the General was obviously reluctant to stay very long. No, he insisted, he didn't want any food or drink. The General took him back to his billet. Sometime later, Stella learned that he had been killed shortly after the landing.

At one point, General Graham introduced her to some senior American officers, including Lt General Omar Bradley, the US Army general in command of all US ground forces. Bradley took Stella's hand and thanked her profusely for coming. But he didn't let go. 'I could feel him shaking and I knew why: these men had the knowledge that 30 to 40 per cent of the men under their command would go. They were top men in charge of thousands of lives: they had to contend with that fact, they knew the likelihood of that happening. I didn't draw away.'

After a few moments, however, he did release his hand, turned and introduced Stella to another American officer, Major General Clarence Huebner, Commander of the US 1st Infantry Division, who would eventually lead the 1st on the assault on Omaha Beach. Stella noted that unlike Bradley, he seemed calm, his feelings under control. Not long after that, the pair left to get back to their ship.

Some of the other women at the party were in US uniform, dancing the jitterbug, but they only stayed for an hour or so.

As the evening progressed, there were a few tense moments when nerves started to fray. One officer proudly produced a family photo to show to Stella. The officer seated next to him abruptly stood up, excused himself, and left. Stella noticed the other men's dismay at this and quickly launched into a conversation about a visit to the National Gallery. It worked. The tension eased. Then the Major General reappeared and asked Stella if she'd care to dance. The band played a waltz and the pair danced, leaving the floor to accompanying applause.

Just before midnight the party ended and, as arranged, the Major General escorted her home in the jeep. He had, he said, been very grateful for Stella's composure that evening. The party had gone extremely well. Then, in the back of the jeep, he asked Stella if he could put his arms around her. 'I said yes; I realized he needed the close human contact.' Then his head dropped onto her shoulder, his body shaking with emotion. 'He held me as though he was clutching for dear life onto a lifebelt on the sea and I was his anchor,' recalled Stella, stunned at the depth of emotion, from a man who commanded the lives of thousands of others. Eventually, he regained his composure and dropped her off at her digs, courteously saying goodbye, with all-too-apparent gratitude.

At that moment, Stella understood that, even for powerful and experienced men like the Major General, the enormity of the task ahead was unnerving, and that the prospect of losing many more young lives in battle was a heavy weight to bear. Yes, this was war, and this was their role as military leaders, but after all, they were only human. 'It was like I was comforting one of my brothers. In a way, I behaved as I would if it had been one of them, a family matter. These men were strangers to me but I didn't treat them that way, I treated them like older brothers.'

The next day Stella took a long bike ride for most of the day, giving her a chance to absorb the events of the previous evening. On Monday, at work, her colleagues accepted her account of what she told them was a party for a group of British and American troops: talk of the food and the dancing satisfied their curiosity. Later that evening, of course, all attention was focused on the invasion itself, which she witnessed with everyone else as wave after wave of aircraft and gliders converged in the night sky above Winchester, heading towards the coast and France.

Stella didn't reveal what happened that night of the secret D-Day party for many years. After the war, she left Supermarine, got married, became Stella Rutter, and had two daughters – but her family knew nothing of her wartime secret. Only nearly seventy years later did she tell her story of that secret party. 'By signing that Secrets Act you gave your life to this country. Few people realize the enormity of that.'

## D-DAY 1944

Although limited planning for the invasion of Europe took place soon after the evacuation of Dunkirk in 1940, detailed preparations for 'Operation Overlord' did not begin until late 1943. A command team led by American

General Dwight D. Eisenhower was formed in December 1943 to plan the naval, air and land operations.

Deception campaigns were developed to draw German attention and strength away from Normandy. To build up resources for the invasion, British factories increased production and in the first half of 1944 approximately 9 million tons of supplies and equipment crossed the Atlantic from North America to Britain.

By 1944, over 2 million troops from over twelve countries were in Britain in preparation for the invasion. D-Day was made possible because of Allied efforts across all fronts both before and after June 1944. On D-Day itself, Allied forces consisted primarily of American, British and Canadian troops but also included Australian, Belgian, Czech, Dutch, French, Greek, New Zealand, Norwegian, Rhodesian and Polish naval, air and ground support.

The Spitfire provided crucial air support for the D-Day landings. The latest Mark IX had 1,720 horsepower engine and was equipped with both 20 mm cannon and .50 calibre machine-guns. Many were also adapted for fighter-bombers to carry out attacks on German ground forces.

Overlord Operation did not bring an end to the war in Europe. But it did begin the process through which victory was eventually achieved.

## Bittersweet Memories

Ken Hone was born in 1922, in a village near Morriston, Swansea. When war broke out, Ken was seventeen. He wanted to fly, and was soon accepted for flying training by the RAF. But during a medical examination, the doctors discovered a problem with his left eye. So he opted to train as a fitter.

'I wound up at a training school in Weston-super-Mare in 1941. Then I was posted, as a flight mechanic, to Little Rissington in Gloucestershire where they flew the Oxfords. Then to Innsworth, near Gloucester, for four months' fitter training. By then I was a LAC [Leading Aircraftsman], a fitter on engines.'

Ken started repairing Spitfires at the Central Gunnery School, RAF Sutton Bridge, Lincolnshire. 'You were learning new techniques all the time and it was hard work – 7 a.m. to 8 p.m. – working on the single-seater Spits and other planes. The first time I worked on one, I was a bit apprehensive. I was very much in awe of the senior technicians, the lads who'd joined the RAF earlier. They were very well trained. It was obvious the pilots depended on them. Anyone who was in the RAF before the war started, they were excellent technicians. My lot, on the other hand, were just a bunch of kids not long out of training.

'As a flight mechanic, it's all checks, oil and water, but as a fitter, it could be a day's work, removing an engine, changing a propeller in the maintenance hangar.' Sutton Bridge, Ken recalled, was tough at first. 'The aerodrome was a mile away from town – where the cookhouse was located. So you always wound up not having any breakfast.

You relied on the NAAFI wagon [a wartime mobile canteen selling cigarettes and snacks] while you worked – we'd be starving. At 8 o' clock, when you'd finished, you'd walk that mile for your evening meal – if you weren't too shattered.

'This situation went on for months and we were pretty dissatisfied with it. In the Forces you couldn't go on strike, but we made the point that we were tired. We stopped work, sat around and in the end they had to work out for themselves why we were so tired! Then they altered it all and we got less working hours.'

Ken decided to volunteer for an overseas posting. In 1943, he was posted to Italy. Initially he worked on a mobile RSU (Repair and Salvage Unit). 'I arrived in Naples by troop ship, *The Queen of Bermuda*, with 5,000 RAF personnel landing there, all to be dispersed with the various squadrons.' The RSU was made up of a group of technicians plus all the equipment needed for recovery of crashed or damaged Spitfires. There was a Coles Crane [for lifting the Spitfires] and a long-bodied lorry – they called it "the Queen Mary" – to carry the Spitfires as well as a normal truck for the rest of the equipment. There was a fitter, a rigger, an electrician, a driver for the Coles Crane and a truck driver.

'Then we were started moving around to recover any crashed aircraft: we were travelling south to north, up the mainland of Italy, following the 8th Army, collecting the crashed Spits: we had to get to them, gather whatever we could before the Germans did. There were groups of us repair and salvage units doing this all over the place in Italy – and there were vast depots where they took all the bits and pieces.'

## THE DEFENCE OF MALTA, 1942

Malta was a key strategic Allied base in wartime. Axis forces laid siege to the island and attacked British supply ships. Stocks were running dangerously low and the RAF called for reinforcements. Over that summer of 1942, hundreds of Spitfire Mark Vbs and Mark Vcs were shipped in by aircraft carriers – this was one of the first times the Spitfire had been deployed outside the UK. These improved Spitfires had a top speed of 371 mph and were armed with powerful 20 mm cannons and four .303 Browning machine guns. The Spitfires proved decisive in gaining air superiority and the siege was broken. Malta then became an important base for supplying British troops in Africa and launching future attacks on Italy.

Ken's RSU made its way up to Rome, then Florence. Just outside Florence he was told he was being posted to 185 Squadron, a fighter-bomber squadron which had taken part in the fierce air battles over Malta, later flying sweeps over Sicily and moving to Italy in 1944, supporting the Allied advance up the length of Italy. This, Ken recalled, was a different life for him in those concluding months of the war, January to April 1945. 'We had between sixteen and eighteen Spits to look after at Pontedera, in between Pisa and Florence, working mostly on Mark VIIIs. We were lucky. 185 was a very friendly squadron. We were living under canvas all the time I was there – it had snowed that

Christmas, the first time in that part of Italy for forty years – and the lads would take a lot of photos when they went out on a raid. I remember them bringing them into the Mess tent to show us. We'd also play cricket and rugby in between the tents – on one occasion at 2 a.m.!'

There was no 'them and us' between the pilots and the ground crew. 'If I did a maintenance job on a Spit, one of the pilots had to test it afterwards. I'd wander into the crew tent and ask for a "driver". Maybe some didn't like you using that word but it was all done with good humour. We didn't discuss what was going on with the war, not in any detail.

'On one action, we were on one side of a hill and the Germans were camped on the other side. It was explained to us by the CO that our lads were doing a raid – they'd be dive-bombing it at mealtime. Later on, the lads brought us a film of that. I think it was one of the last major jobs the squadron had.'

Yet there was one situation in those last months that Ken would never forget. 'A new lad came onto the squadron, he was about nineteen or twenty. I went to see him off, into the pilot's seat, but I felt a bit concerned about him. Just a sixth sense you get.'

Ken had never tried to do anything like this before, yet somehow he felt compelled to try to give the young lad some help. 'I sat on the wing as he taxied to the end of the runway. Then I spoke to him, standing on the wing. I suggested that if he didn't want to take off, I would classify the aircraft as unserviceable, take it back to dispersal. I could see he was very nervous. He just shook his head and then he went off.'

The young pilot didn't come back. 'They found his plane

in a river. It was his first trip on a squadron in a war zone. His temperament just wasn't right. He'd have been one of the last ones to be killed in the squadron.'

Ken had, of course, witnessed other disasters since joining the RAF. 'At Little Riss, I'd seen two Oxfords collide in the dark, lads on navigation training.' On another occasion, at Pontedera, Ken got chatting to the new Squadron Leader. 'I asked him what he'd do when war ended. "Dunno," he told me. "I used to ride a bike for Liptons," he said.' (Liptons was a large chain of grocery stores.) 'Then he got killed in a Spit while dive bombing.'

By the time 185 Squadron had moved north to the area around the River Po the announcement came: the war was over. 'At the end, we got the order: "Dig some trenches". We dug the trenches and we filled them up with all our equipment. We dumped the lot. That was the end of 185 Squadron. Then we were reclassified as 55 Squadron and moved to Athens in September 1945. It was all over.'

Ken was finally demobbed in September 1946. He got married almost immediately afterwards and had three children. Later he divorced and moved south, working as an engineer at Vauxhall in Luton for twenty-three years until it closed down. Looking back on the war, he felt there was no real logic to any of it. They all learned to live for the day, no more. 'There was no tomorrow. You just hoped there was. Every day your mates went out, some didn't come back. You just got on with your life. Made the most of it.'

# Key Figures

## The Designers

### Reginald Joseph Mitchell (known as 'RJ'), CBE, FRAes.
### Chief Designer, Supermarine Aviation Works
### (1895–1937)

R. J. Mitchell was born in Talke, a village near Stoke-on-Trent. As a teenager he would spend hours building and flying model aircraft. He left school at sixteen to start an engineering apprenticeship at a firm called Kerr Stuart, where he began working in the drawing office after completing his apprenticeship.

At twenty-two he joined Supermarine Aviation Works at Woolston, Southampton. Two years later he was promoted to Chief Designer and became heavily involved in designing high-speed aircraft, including racing planes. Between 1920 and 1936 he designed twenty-four different types of aircraft including flying boats and bombers. He was also responsible for several award-winning designs, including two that broke air speed records for the Schneider Trophy in 1929 and 1931. His design for the Spitfire – highly manoeuvrable and built for speed – was revolutionary and the iconic elliptical wing, designed by Mitchell to give a warning judder before an impending engine stall, went on to save many pilot's lives.

Despite serious illness, Mitchell resisted all efforts to get him to rest, determined to meet the need for a fighter aircraft which could perform on equal terms with the German Luftwaffe. He knew that the engine for this fighter plane needed to be designed and built to suit the plane, rather than building an airframe around the engine. As a result, Rolls-Royce produced the now famous Merlin engine in 1936 followed by the Griffon engine in 1939.

In a letter to Mitchell's widow, written after his death in 1937, Viscount Swinton, Secretary of State for Air, wrote: 'His was real genius. His work is his memorial.'

### Joseph 'Joe' Smith, CBE, Supermarine Designer (1897–1956)

Joseph Smith, Supermarine's Chief Draughtsman, took over as Chief Designer after Mitchell died and oversaw the development of the Spitfire throughout the Second World War. Strongly focused in the belief that the Spitfire's development potential would continue through the war years, his contribution to the success of the Spitfire and his dedicated leadership of the Supermarine design team were invaluable. While Mitchell was an extremely clever designer and innovator, Smith proved to be the pragmatic engineer who could oversee development and make it all work.

One of his most significant achievements was overseeing

the introduction of the Rolls-Royce Griffon-engined series of Spitfires, increasing their speed and altitude capabilities beyond those of the Merlin-engined Spitfires. Thanks to Smith's leadership, many innovations to the earlier Spitfire were eventually brought in, including the installations of cameras and improved armaments.

Smith's career began with an apprenticeship with the Austin Motor Company at Longbridge, near Birmingham. He served with the Royal Naval Volunteer Reserve during the First World War and, following a short period as a junior draughtsman in Austin's aviation department, in 1921 he moved to the aviation department of Vickers-Armstrongs (Vickers acquired Supermarine Aviation Works in 1928) as a senior draughtsman in their drawing office. He was subsequently promoted to Chief Draughtsman five years later, and became Chief Designer in 1937 after Mitchell's death.

After the war, Smith was appointed a special director of Vickers-Armstrongs and was awarded the CBE in 1945. He died in February 1956 aged fifty-eight.

## The Test Pilots

### Joseph 'Mutt' Summers, CBE, the man who made the first ever Spitfire flight (1904–54)

Summers' aviation career began in 1924, aged twenty-one, when he was granted a short service commission with the RAF. He then spent six months with 29 Squadron before working at the Royal Aircraft Establishment, where he worked as a test pilot for five years.

He joined Vickers Aviation as their Chief Test Pilot in 1929 and a year later became Chief Test Pilot at Supermarine Aviation Works. Known for his quick reflexes and sophisticated image (he spoke fluent German and, pre-war, was in regular contact with Luftwaffe pilots) it was said he had the ability to fly virtually anything.

The nickname 'Mutt' came from his early RAF habit of urinating before take-off on a small rear wheel of the plane he was testing, like a dog marking its territory. In fact, he did it because he believed a full bladder could prove lethal in a crash.

When he left the plane after that first eight-minute flight, he was famously reported as saying, 'I don't want anything touched.' It was taken quite literally by the press at the time, and was partly responsible for the public perception of the Spitfire as the perfect fighter plane. In fact, what he really meant was he wanted to fly it again with the controls and everything else left untouched by anyone until the next flight.

During the war, Summers became a supervising RAF flight tester and went on to fly Britain's first ever postwar airliner, the Vickers VC1 Nene-Viking. He clocked up 5,600 flying hours and tested around 366 different types of plane. He died, aged fifty, in March 1954 following colon surgery.

### Jeffrey 'Mr Spitfire' Quill, OBE, AFC, FRAeS, Supermarine Senior Test Pilot who flew every variant of the Spitfire and Seafire (1913–96)

Quill grew up in Littlehampton, Sussex, son of an Irish engineer and the youngest of five children. In 1926, he started his secondary education at Lancing College, overlooking Shoreham aerodrome – and his fascination with the aerial activity overhead led to a non-commissioned career with the RAF in 1931.

In 1932, he joined RAF 17 Squadron at Upavon, flying Bristol Bulldog fighters. A year later he was posted to the Meteorological Flight section at Duxford, flying in open-cockpit Siskin (a single-seater fighter plane of the 1920s) to collect weather report data. He joined Vickers Supermarine in January 1936 as Summers' assistant, before being promoted to Senior Test Pilot.

Articulate, brave and highly intelligent, he was posted to 65 Squadron in August and September 1940 to test the Spitfire in combat. He flew with the squadron from Hornchurch, Essex, during the Battle of Britain and is recorded to have shot at a BF 109. This flying experience gave him valuable insight into the plane's handling and inspired ideas on improvements that could be made to the Spitfire.

Amongst other things, combat showed Quill that pilots were getting shot down by an enemy they could not see: the optical qualities of the windscreen side panels were defective and the lines of the rear fuselage and the canopy impeded rear vision. The design was changed.

His reputation as a superb troubleshooter led to another five-month period away from test piloting in 1943 when he was commissioned into the Royal Navy to advise on modifications to the Supermarine Seafire, which was experiencing problems with aircraft carrier landings: his reports led to essential changes for future productions of Seafires and training of its pilots.

At the end of the war, Quill continued to test new aircraft until a flying incident led to him losing consciousness at 40,000 feet. He managed to land safely but medical checks revealed that his health had suffered unduly following sixteen years of test piloting, often at high altitude and without oxygen. He moved into a desk job, initially with Vickers-Armstrongs, then as military aircraft marketing executive for the British Aircraft Corporation. He continued to fly a Mark V Spitfire at aviation shows until his last Spitfire flight in 1960, though he did not formally retire until 1978. He later wrote two books chronicling the Spitfire and its legacy. He died, aged eighty-three, in February 1996.

### Alexander Henshaw, MBE, Chief Production Test Pilot at Castle Bromwich (1912–2007)

The son of a wealthy businessman and educated at Lincoln Grammar School, Henshaw was fascinated by motorcycles and flying from a very early age. In 1932, his father funded flying lessons for his son, later buying him a de Havilland Gypsy Moth.

It proved to be a good investment. In 1938, Henshaw won the prestigious King's Cup air race and the following year he made a record breaking solo flight from Gravesend in Kent to Cape Town and back.

With war imminent, he initially volunteered to join the RAF but was invited to join Vickers-Armstrongs as a test pilot at Weybridge, Surrey. Initially, Henshaw tested Wellingtons and the Walrus (the early seaplane designed by R. J. Mitchell) but found this work unsatisfactory. Then he met Jeffrey Quill, Supermarine's Senior Test Pilot, who offered him a job.

At first, Henshaw flew Spitfires at Supermarine's Southampton factory. Then, in June 1940, he moved to the Vickers Supermarine factory at Castle Bromwich as Chief Production Test Pilot for Spitfires and Lancasters, overseeing a team of twenty-five. Between 1940 and 1945 he test flew 2,360 Spitfires and Seafires, sometimes testing twenty planes in a single day. Flights didn't always go according to plan, and on one occasion Henshaw was forced out of his Spitfire when the engine exploded and he was thrown out of the plane by the blast. He became entangled in his torn parachute, but the parachute held together on the descent and he managed to land safely.

Henshaw was sometimes required to demonstrate the Spitfire in flight in front of visiting VIPs. His aerial display so enthralled Winston Churchill that the great man kept his train for the return journey waiting while he chatted to the pilot.

After the war, Henshaw joined his family's farming business and remained much in demand in the aviation world at events and presentations. Tough-minded but approachable, he took much interest in promoting 'air-mindedness' amongst the young. In 2006, to mark the seventieth anniversary of the first Spitfire flight, he flew as a passenger over Southampton in a two-seater Spitfire, at one point briefly taking the controls. His pilot noted that the ninety-three-year-old could have landed the aircraft were it not for the somewhat prohibitive insurance restrictions. Henshaw died in February 2007, aged ninety-four.

# Further Reading

Alexander, Kristen, *Australia's Few and the Battle of Britain*, Pen & Sword Aviation, 2015.

Hill, Alison, *Sisters in Spitfires*, Indigo Dreams Publishing, 2015.

Nicholson, Virginia, *Millions Like Us: Women's Lives During the Second World War*, Penguin, 2011.

Price, Dr Alfred, *The Spitfire Story*, Haynes Publishing, 2010.

Spencer, Lesley and Terence, *Living Dangerously*, Percival Publications, 2002.

Wellum, Geoffrey, *First Light*, Penguin, 2002.

# Acknowledgements

A very big thank you to Stephen Greensted, Deborah Scarfe, Ivor Warne, Ken and Maureen Hone, Martin Bisiker at Legasee, Mick Oakey at The Aviation Historian, Matt Jones at Boultbee Flight Academy, Kristen Alexander, Gareth Phipps, Cara Spencer, Lyndi Roberts, David Gash, Dilip Sarkar, Lou-Lou Troup, Alan Nicholl, Mark Hillier, Mark Harrison, Alison Hill, Daniel Swan, Geoff Simpson, James Carter, Rebecca Fletcher at Birmingham Museums Trust, Michael Mockford, Jacky Rees, Carolyn Grace (www.ml407.co.uk) and Richard Henriquez.

My sincere thanks, too, to the research teams at RAF Museum, Imperial War Museums, London and Duxford, and Solent Sky Museum, Southampton.

# Picture Credits

(Photo of Geoffrey Wellum in Introduction: IWM HU 112488)

Page 1: IWM CH 19

Page 2: (top) IWM A 1813, (middle) Art.IWM PST 8261, (bottom) H. F. Davis / Stringer / Getty Images

Page 3: (top) Art.IWM ART LD 1550, (middle) IWM Q 80649, (bottom) IWM H 14259

Page 4: Photos courtesy of Christine Haig

Page 5: (top left) Art.IWM PST 14281, (top right) Art.IWM PST 14229, (bottom) IWM HU 89805

Page 6: (top) IWM E(MOS) 1, (middle) IWM HU 93074, (bottom) Andy R. Annable

Page 7: (top) IWM H 14264, (bottom) IWM CH 1368

Page 8: (top) IWM CH 7698, (middle) IWM CH 7346, (bottom) CH 8945

Page 9: (top left) IWM CH 2064, (top right) IWM TR 2145, (middle) IWM CH 12752, (bottom) IWM CH 1398

Page 10: (top) © Matt Jones, (bottom) © Keith Larby / Alamy

Page 11: (top) © John M. Dibbs, (bottom) © Andy R. Annable

Page 12: (top) IWM MH 13763, (middle) E(MOS) 1325, (bottom left) IWM CH 1459, (bottom right) IWM CH 8010

# Index